We celebrate the release of our daughter's book, *She's Still There*. With uncanny honesty, vulnerability, and spiritual insight, Chrystal will lead you on an exciting journey to rescue the girl in you. This groundbreaking work will reconnect you to the joyful and, yes, sometimes tearful discovery of the person God created you to be.

—DRS. TONY AND LOIS EVANS

My witty and wise friend Chrystal will help you rediscover your lost dreams and uncover a renewed passion for moving forward. She knows what you're feeling, but even better, she reveals the decisions you can make to get back on track.

—LYSA TERKEURST, *New York Times* bestselling author; president, Proverbs 31 Ministries

A woman's resurrection journey is an important and powerful conversation to have, even for a husband and wife. *She's Still There* is a tool to aid every woman in cultivating her dreams, reigniting her passions, and reviving her heart. Chrystal's message breathes life into the girl who needs a fresh start. A renewed sense of hope and purpose is just a page away.

—KIRK AND TAMMY FRANKLIN, Grammy Award–winning artist, author

If you're a woman who's felt lost, buried, overlooked, or unsure of her identity, this book is written for you. If you've ever wondered, "Where did I go? What happened to the girl I thought I'd be?" Chrystal offers the tender comfort of a good friend as well as the swift kick in the pants you need to rise up, own your story, and rescue the buried parts of the girl who is longing to come to life. While it can be hard to own the rocky parts of your story, *She's Still There* encourages you to believe that you are a soul uniquely designed by God for a purpose, and gives you the tools you need to rescue the best of the girl in you.

—CHRISTINE CAINE, founder, A21 and Propel Women

She's Still There will help women get out the box of fear and shame and walk in their God given freedom! This is a bold, honest, and lifechanging book!

—ERICA CAMPBELL, Grammy Award–winning artist, radio host

Chrystal is a fierce lover of God and people. Courage and empathy pour out of this woman. Prepare to be loved and challenged in these words.

—JENNIE ALLEN, visionary and founder, IF:Gathering; author, *Nothing to Prove*

What you're still looking for? Is right here in your hands. What you're still hoping to find? Begins with turning these pages. What you're still holding out for? You're holding onto right now. Everything that girl you once were ever dreamed of, prayed for, imagined? That girl? She's still there. And you can still believe. Chrystal's words are like a healing balm, a strengthening iron, and an envisioning hope. She is one wise guide, gentle counsellor, and needed friend in your journey to find your way back to what you once hoped for. Your soul is begging you to begin.

—ANN VOSKAMP, *New York Times* bestselling author,
The Broken Way and *One Thousand Gifts*

Have you ever met one of those women who made you feel like a friend you could never let go of from the moment you meet? That's what happened when I met Chrystal, and that's what will happen to you the moment you crack open this book. Prepare to be comforted and transformed by a woman who embodies the love of God.

—SARAH JAKES ROBERTS, author; copastor, One Church LA

What I love about *She's Still There*? Chrystal tells the truth, holding nothing back. She's honest about her struggles and compassionate about ours. Her wisdom is hard earned and generously shared, and her suggestions are both practical and purposeful. Her wry humor comes through, but so does her heart for God. Chrystal writes from a place of passion and conviction, and so gives her sisters a beautiful gift: freedom. Open it, my friend. You won't be disappointed!

—LIZ CURTIS HIGGS, author, bestselling *Bad Girls of the Bible*

Surprisingly poignant. Startlingly transparent. Stunningly insightful. Chrystal touched me deeply as I read her milestone book, which is destined to set women free on a deep and meaningful level. Rarely have I read a book so down-to-earth with such heavenly wisdom. Don't miss this amazing book!

—BRUCE WILKINSON, president, Teach Every Nation

Chrystal shares her story with an intimacy that makes the reader feel as if they are sitting down for coffee with her. The truth and vulnerability of Chrystal's story are packed with wisdom and steps to help anyone regain or discover for the first time the woman they were meant to be. As I devoured Chrystal's words, I felt as though she were sitting across from me at a coffee shop. She's the friend we all want. The friend who is real and vulnerable with you and constantly points you to the truth. If you are a woman, this book needs to be in your hands!

—JAMIE IVEY, podcast host, *The Happy Hour with Jamie Ivey*

Chrystal is honest, hilarious, and full of encouragement for any of us who have looked up and realized life hasn't gone exactly the way we planned. And isn't that all of us? *She's Still There* is refreshing in its transparency and encouraging in its authenticity. Chrystal reminds us that God never loses sight of us even when we lose sight of ourselves and is always working all things together for our good. You will find yourself sighing with relief, wiping away a few tears, and turning the final page knowing how much you are loved.

—**MELANIE SHANKLE**, author, *New York Times* bestselling *Nobody's Cuter Than You*

Chrystal writes with the passion and wisdom of a woman who has lived fully and gleaned every lesson life has to offer. *She's Still There* is a joy to read and an inspiration for any woman who is ready to break out of a rut and step fully into the abundant life for which she was created.

—**VALORIE BURTON**, founder, The CaPP Institute; author, bestselling *Successful Women Think Differently*

If you're stuck in a life you never imagined and fear you've lost the best parts of yourself along the way, you're not alone. I've been there, more than once. It's crushing, painful. But here's the good news: you're holding a lifeline your hands. Through the rich pages of *She's Still There*, Chrystal offers honest revelation, warm companionship, and hope-filled truth to help you rediscover the best parts of your life—and yourself.

—**MICHELE CUSHATT**, author, *I Am: A 60-Day Journey to Knowing Who You Are Because of Who He Is*

Chrystal puts her finger on our inner struggles as she shares stories of her life. Her heartfelt experiences lead us to courage, faith, and wisdom to live well. Chrystal's powerful messages always inspire me.

—**SALLY CLARKSON**, author, *Different* and *The Lifegiving Home*

I love Chrystal's raw transparency and comical storytelling as she shares from her heart stories of God's amazing work in her life. Through *She's Still There*, you'll be reminded and encouraged that in life's ups and downs, good decisions and mistakes, God uses it all for a greater purpose. Be who God created you to be; you're perfect that way!

—**ANGELA PERRITT**, founder and director, LoveGodGreatly.com; coauthor, *You Are Loved and You Are Forgiven*

I love this book. And I love Chrystal. She's managed to fill each page with hard-fought wisdom and insight. Far too many of us live with our unresolved issues buried beneath the surface, but in a place that wreaks havoc on our souls and skews our perspective. God wants to unearth the things we've buried so he can heal and reveal, correct and redirect, and, ultimately, restore us. No matter where you've been, what you've done, or what's been done to you, God can redeem it if you'll trust him and give him access to your story. Dig in to the material here with expectancy and vulnerability. God is about to do a *new* thing in you!

—**SUSIE LARSON,** national speaker; talk radio host;
author, *Your Powerful Prayers*

Chrystal cheers us on and calls us out, sharing her unexpected journey, while showing us how to value our souls, accept our processes, refocus our thoughts, and reaffirm our worth as women God created for a purpose we may not yet know, but one worth discovering! Packed with me-too stories, real-life application, and humorous-yet-convicting truth, *She's Still There* is a message every women needs. Grab a copy for yourself and a friend!

—**RENEE SWOPE,** author, *A Confident Heart*

Chrystal is a woman who has experienced brokenness, which gives her a huge heart for women who are in the same place. Read this work, which is a reflection of God's putting her back together as he puts you back together.

—**DR. ERIC MASON,** founder and pastor,
Epiphany Fellowship, Philadelphia

Chrystal's passion for helping women of all generations challenges me as a blogger, mother, and boss. In *She's Still There*, Chrystal encourages women to deeply engage in their own stories through healing of the past and embracing the present. If you are trying to resist drifting off course in your life, this book will help you find the purpose God has for you.

—**SUSAN MERRILL,** founder, iMOM;
author, *The Passionate Mom*

SHE'S
STILL
THERE

SHE'S STILL THERE

Rescuing the Girl in You

CHRYSTAL EVANS HURST

ZONDERVAN®

ZONDERVAN

She's Still There
Copyright © 2017 by Chrystal Evans Hurst

Requests for information should be addressed to:
Zondervan, *3900 Sparks Dr. SE, Grand Rapids, Michigan 49546*

Library of Congress Cataloging-in-Publication Data

ISBN 978-0-310-34781-1 (softcover)

ISBN 978-0-310-35049-1 (audio)

ISBN 978-0-310-34806-1 (ebook)

Unless otherwise noted, Scripture quotations are taken from The Holy Bible, New International Version®, NIV®. Copyright © 1973, 1978, 1984, 2011 by Biblica, Inc.® Used by permission of Zondervan. All rights reserved worldwide. www.Zondervan.com. The "NIV" and "New International Version" are trademarks registered in the United States Patent and Trademark Office by Biblica, Inc.®

Scripture quotations marked AMP are from the Amplified® Bible. Copyright © 1954, 1958, 1962, 1964, 1965, 1987 by The Lockman Foundation. Used by permission. (www.Lockman.org).

Scripture quotations marked CEB are from the Common English Bible. Copyright © 2011 Common English Bible.

Scripture quotations marked CEV are from the Contemporary English Version. Copyright © 1991, 1992, 1995 by American Bible Society. Used by permission.

Scripture quotations marked ESV are from the ESV® Bible (The Holy Bible, English Standard Version®). Copyright © 2001 by Crossway, a publishing ministry of Good News Publishers. Used by permission. All rights reserved.

Scripture quotations marked KJV are from the King James Version. Public domain.

Scripture quotations marked NASB are from New American Standard Bible®. Copyright © 1960, 1962, 1963, 1968, 1971, 1972, 1973, 1975, 1977, 1995 by The Lockman Foundation. Used by permission. (www.Lockman.org).

Scripture quotations marked NKJV are from the New King James Version®. © 1982 by Thomas Nelson. Used by permission. All rights reserved.

Scripture quotations marked NLT are from the Holy Bible, New Living Translation. © 1996, 2004, 2007, 2013, 2015 by Tyndale House Foundation. Used by permission of Tyndale House Publishers, Inc., Carol Stream, Illinois 60188. All rights reserved.

Any Internet addresses (websites, blogs, etc.) and telephone numbers in this book are offered as a resource. They are not intended in any way to be or imply an endorsement by Zondervan, nor does Zondervan vouch for the content of these sites and numbers for the life of this book.

Cover illustrations: AlienValley / Creative Market
Interior design: Kait Lamphere

First printing June 2017 / Printed in the United States of America

To my original sister circle—my mother, Lois; my sister Priscilla; my aunt Elizabeth; and my friend Michelle—who never let me forget that I was worth the work of the rescue and who never stopped believing that the best of the girl in me was still there

And to my oldest daughter, Kariss, who asked me the hard question to which I pray this book is the answer

CONTENTS

FOREWORD

I unpacked my travel bag this week.

I guess there's nothing novel about that, unless you take into account that it came back with me from travels four weeks earlier. That's right. *Four weeks.* Despite my best intentions to unload and clean away all the luggage that returned with us from family vacation, I hadn't been able to get it all done. Or maybe I just hadn't wanted to. Honestly, it seemed like the suitcases had multiplied on the flight back, now that they carried the loads of dirty laundry that Momma (that's me) would need to clean.

But finally, I got to the last bag. My bag. The only one remaining in the heap of belongings that returned with us. I finally dug into it one night after getting my sons to bed and putting my stuff away. And there, wedged in between my running shoes and my dirty jeans, was the gift.

I'd loved receiving it while we'd been away. A kind woman I'd only just met had placed it in my hands with a smile and with specific, personal, uncomplicated instructions: "Enjoy it," she'd said. And I had. For the remainder of our trip. It was just a little token, a delectable indulgence that I'd used and then forgotten after burying it in my luggage for the ride home. Discovering it now, after all this time, brought a smile to my face. I was so glad to lay claim to it once again. So I put it where it belonged—out in the open where I wouldn't forget about it again and could do with it exactly what I'd been instructed to do: enjoy it.

As I think back on that gift and that moment, it prompts me to tell you something important: this book is an invitation to enjoy something too.

Chrystal Hurst has done a masterful job of penning a resource that is less a book to read and more a tool to employ. It's not an instruction manual as much as it is a Phillips-head screwdriver, opening things locked away and in need of freedom. It's also a swift kick in the hind parts for women like you and me who've left our lives unattended far too long, packed to the brim with the mundane stuff of eight-to-five living, stuff that's made us mindless and sterile and unfeeling, stuff that multiplies until it swallows us whole.

Each page will take the numbness away from your emotional limbs and spark a flame in your soul to mine the treasure you've been given by God. It will shine a spotlight on the clutter in your life that you've been too busy or too tired or too disinterested to unpack so that you can get to the good stuff. The priceless stuff. The stuff that makes life worth living.

The gift.

Sure, it's work—and not for sissies, I might add. Unpacking the luggage of life cakes emotional dirt under those French-manicured nails, the ones you've been trying so hard to keep pristine.

But it's worth it.

'Cause there's a gift deep down in there. Usually it's wedged between your running shoes ('cause running from this whole thing always seems easiest) and your dirty laundry ('cause airing it out is much more complicated than just buying new digs). But neither running nor camouflaging will help you recover the gift—the gift of who you really are and who you were really meant to be. Digging deep is the only way to do that.

These carefully crafted, diligently prayed-over pages will encourage you to stop walking around it, ignoring it, or glazing it over. And to just get on with it already.

So I'm asking, Are you game?

Well, me too.

Chrystal is brave. Not because she wrote this book but because she lives it. I know this to be true, not because I've read about her in some blog post or have seen her speak at a convention with thousands of women wearing white skinny jeans and carrying colored pens for notetaking in their bejeweled journals. I know it because I've seen it. I've seen her. Up close. Like with a magnifying glass.

She's my big sister. I mean, biologically.

And that's why I can recommend this resource to you with steely confidence and enthusiasm. This woman has done the work of digging deep and finding the gift of her true self that got masked by the nitty-gritty of life. I'm not just talking dishes, diapers, and laundry. I'm talking health scares and crippling financial strain and dashed dreams. The digging was deep and difficult, the kind that required her to wear sweatpants and baggy T-shirts, 'cause skinny jeans weren't made for this kind of thing. It was hard and tiring and sometimes even brutal, but it was necessary and gratifying. And she did it (and is still doing it). She got her hands on the treasure of herself.

And once she did, she never let go. And neither will you. The gift of yourself is too valuable a treasure to hold loosely.

This is the resource you and I have been waiting on, the one we need to remind us that *She's Still There*. Better yet, it will give you the confidence to believe it and the courage to get up and go at once to bring her back out into the open. Where she belongs.

Oh, and it will do something more. It will cup its hand toward your ear and whisper to your listening soul, "Enjoy it."

Bless you as you read.

—Priscilla Shirer

ACKNOWLEDGMENTS

One year. Thinking. Praying. Crying. Coffee. Sweet tea. Protein drinks. Late nights. Early mornings. And a few all-nighters. Starbucks. Panera. TGI Friday's. Write. Erase. Write again. Word. Scrivener. Red ink on printed paper.

A publishing family that fielded my many questions and supported me even when I went way over my word count.

A writing coach who didn't know how much work she was in for but never once lost her enthusiasm. Three heaven-sent helpers who read every word (or had every word read to them) and spent hours helping me process my thoughts. Friends—their ears, their time, their opinions.

Family—they know me, they've helped me, they care about what I have to say. My sister's beautiful gift of encouragement. My brother's LA apartment and fierce faith in my idea. My other brother's superb wit and "bottom line" processing.

My mom's couch. Her food. Her friendship. My dad's brain. His time. His legacy. The patience, hugs, and kisses from my fabulous five kids, my son-in-love, and my supersnuggable granddaughter. My husband's quiet sacrifice, steadfast support, and love.

Me. Hoping that I'd get to do it. Thinking I couldn't do it. Realizing it was my destiny to do it. It's time—time to share the message of my heart.

AN OPEN LETTER TO MY READER

I love Jesus.

Let me just say that up front because I know some of you will be reading these pages looking for lots of talk about Him. But while this book is about what I've learned while sometimes walking with Him— and sometimes not—this book is more about my experiences and what God has allowed me to learn. Sometimes I've learned because the school of hard knocks is a tough teacher, but a good one. Sometimes I've learned because I've chosen common sense. Many times I've learned because I decided to act as if I believed God's Word is true.

In this book, you will find the thread of God's story in my life and the lessons He has taught me. You will find a lot of my personal story. You will find plenty of encouragement for you as I share principles I've learned. You will find Scripture, particularly at the end of each chapter, if you want to dig deeper. If you want to go even farther, there is a separate Bible study to dive into. But most of this book is written just the way I would talk to you if you met me for an early morning cup of coffee. During that coffee shop conversation, I would hope that you feel as if you have a friend, someone who understands you and someone who will tell you the truth. As you read the book, my prayer is that you feel the exact same way.

Parts of the words I've written will be gentle and kind. You may cry as you see yourself and your story in these pages. Some parts of this book will leave you smiling and feeling inspired, because I will come alongside you as your cheerleader. But I have to tell you that some of my words will be direct and firm. Why? Because real friends tell their friends the truth, even when it's not easy for them to hear it.

I hope you pause at the end of every chapter for a little R&R. "Reflections for the Rescue" is an opportunity for you to take a break and process your journey as you join me on my own. I encourage you to take that time to journal, think, or pray, choosing to do your part to rescue the girl in you.

My prayer is that at the end of this book you are motivated to get to the business of choosing to believe in the gift of "you." My hope is that you will act as if the girl in you is still there and be willing to do whatever it takes to participate in her rescue. Most important, I pray that you will choose to give the gift of understanding, encouragement, and truth to someone else who needs to believe her life still matters. We girls need each other.

Your partner in the rescue effort,

Chrystal

PART 1

FIGHT FOR YOUR LIFE

I can impress you with my achievements, or I share my struggle and pray that it leads to your transformation.

—*Kirk Franklin*

You cannot amputate your history from your destiny, because that is redemption.

—*Beth Moore*

BREAK A LEG . . . OR TWO

You Are a Masterpiece

G*od, if you would just break both of my legs, that would make every-thing better.*

I was driving down the tollway in Dallas, headed home from another day at work, where I had spent hours stuffed in a cubicle, checking a million boxes with a red pen. My brain was about to explode.

I hated my job.

The clock crawled from the moment I sat in my chair until the time it was reasonable for me to run out the door at the end of the day. It felt as if I were gasping for fresh air.

And that's why I asked God to break my legs.

I made it clear that I didn't want Him to take my life or allow me to be injured in a way that permanently altered my life. And I certainly didn't want an accident that marred my face or scarred me in any way. I just wanted to hit the reset button, and I figured one or two broken legs would do the trick.

In my stressed-out, overwhelmed, off-track mode of thinking, I wished for the shelter of a hospital room—a justifiable excuse for a break—to provide an escape and some time to assess where I'd gotten off track and to formulate a plan for making my life more like I'd imagined it would be. I was like a crazy woman, talking to Him in the car out loud, tears streaming down my face and my heart racing at the thought that He might actually allow me to pray my way right into the hospital.

I hadn't intended to end up in a job I didn't love.

I hadn't intended to be a single parent.

I hadn't intended to have a heart still raw and exposed from the hurt imposed on it by other people.

It had never been my dream to fight my way through the academic challenges and personal struggles of my college years—at that point the most difficult season of my life—only to end up on the other side of the so-called victory of graduation feeling deflated. I had filled my balloon of hope with expectations and dreams only to realize that I had not tied it tightly enough.

And the air had escaped.

As a young, twenty-something-year-old girl, it hadn't been that long since I'd felt full of hope, promise, and excitement. So I was taken by surprise to find I now spent most of my waking hours feeling resentful, hopeless, and miserably bored each and every day.

Where had I gone? Where was the girl who once lived in anticipation of the beauty of her life? How did I lose her? And how would I ever get her back?

I'd love to tell you that in those moments driving down the freeway and thinking like a crazy person, I magically gained clarity on how I'd gotten off track. I'd like to say that I never got off track again.

I'd love to tell you that I figured all of it out right then and that I've had it all figured out since.

The truth is I haven't solved everything. But I have gained an understanding over time, and that's what I want to share with you in these pages.

I want to reassure you that the best of the girl in you is still there. She still has the chance to live her life.

In that moment when I was just short of being delusional—or maybe I was delusional and didn't know it—I didn't recognize my life. Whatever I'd thought my life was going to be, this wasn't it, and I thought what I needed was time out of the rat race—a break or two (pun intended)—to figure things out.

I was off track and didn't know how to get back on except for a desperate plea to God: *do something to help me!*

All I knew was that I was not living *my* life—the life I'd hoped for, the life I'd dreamed of, the life I still desperately wanted to have.

It felt like the girl I wanted to be was dying a slow suffocating death, and I was clueless as to how to help her.

It hadn't always been like that, though.

I recalled moments when my girl felt alive and easily able to breathe.

My parents encouraged me to live with wonder, my teachers gave me the courage to explore, my friends allowed me the chance to play, and my world offered me the opportunity to learn and grow. Fall and spring days were full with homework, school activities, and play with neighborhood friends. The summer months held visits to my grandparents, slumber parties with cousins, and long, boring days with an occasional trip to the library. Whatever didn't satisfy me about my girlhood fired up the desires of my heart, desires I figured I would honor when I was old enough.

You know, when I was "grown and free."

Who knew that escaping childhood meant giving up naps, free room and board, and summers off?

From the vantage point of childhood, I could hope and dream. And I had a picture of what I thought my grown-up life might look like. I imagined my future family, my future career, and the future places I'd live. I still have the paper with the names of my twelve kids written on it. I figured I would either be a teacher or a famous actress and that I'd live close to my family but have a second home near the beach.

Every book I read and every person I met introduced me to more of the world that I could experience. I thought of the people I might one day meet, the places I might one day travel, and things I might one day do. And while I have yet to meet Julia Roberts, explore Australia, or release my own album, I haven't forgotten the thoughts that went through my head before I shifted into adulthood.

My thoughts, dreams, and expectations had room to run.

Don't get me wrong. The picture wasn't always pristine. I haven't forgotten about the hard parts—the cruelty of other kids, the stinging words of some adults, the torrential trip through my teenage years.

My youth wasn't perfect, but less-than-perfect didn't stop me from growing. I accepted my childhood for what it was, part of the process of my progress through life. I leaned into the living, believing that all the beautiful and unpleasant parts of my current and future picture would someday make sense if I just kept going.

I believed in the idea of a masterpiece.

I've believed that all parts of my life—the good, the bad, and the ugly—could come together in the hands of the person who gave me life. I believed through ups and downs that He knew what He was doing and that He could make something beautiful of my life in His time.

That day in that car, I didn't self-destruct. I chose to keep driving. Even while the tears streamed down my face and I cried out to God for help, I kept going for one reason and one reason alone.

I believed my girl was still there.

Even if she seemed lost, invisible, and forgotten, I decided to hope against hope that God could still make a masterpiece out of her.

Maybe you've felt the same way. Maybe you've been a crazy woman like me and begged God to help you fix your life, get unstuck, and get it together. Maybe you've thought long and hard about what extreme measure you could take to stop the pain and heartache.

Maybe you imagined that by now you'd have a career you loved, finances that kept you content, or a marriage made in heaven. Maybe you thought you'd have a house that felt like home, a child who brought you joy, or a deep solid faith you could stand on. Maybe you are tired of waiting on a dream that seems way overdue and possibly unattainable.

It can be puzzling to realize that your very present and real life doesn't resemble your past expectations.

It can be bewildering when your life looks nothing like the life you pictured.

It can be confusing, but it's also common.

Every woman I know has had at least one moment of cognitive dissonance in her life. She comes face to face with the girl she is and compares her with the girl she wanted to be and it just doesn't line up. Or maybe she never knew exactly what she wanted in her life but simply knows deep down that who or where she is now isn't it.

She believes there must be more. And so she's faced with a choice.

She can do nothing and continue in disappointment, shame, frustration, inactivity, or regret.

Or she can recalibrate and get to the business of believing that her life is a work of art.

A masterpiece.

She can choose to be brave enough to believe that a uniquely beautiful life is still hers to have. And she can choose to be bold enough to grab hold of the hope she has for the girl inside. The girl who's still there.

The girl who dreamed of—and deserves—her beautiful life.

Notice I didn't say perfect.

Your life is not going to be perfect.

How do I know? Because I have yet to meet someone who claims a hundred percent perfect life a hundred percent of the time. And I know because my own life hasn't been perfect.

> Be brave enough to believe that a uniquely beautiful life can be yours.

At times, I've witnessed my own life morph unrecognizably into a life that made me sad, desperate, and numb. I drifted away from being the girl of my dreams or simply turned my back on her, pretending that her life didn't matter.

But time and time again, I've sensed her calling me, begging me to answer, to acknowledge her existence and honor the life that is still hers to lead. And I believe.

Her life does matter. And her beautiful life is still possible.

I've learned that the living of that beautiful life takes practice. It takes time to cultivate. I've learned that my picture blends and takes shape as I choose to continue journeying through life, even if I make mistakes or hard times come. I've learned to accept that the process of becoming is a part of my progress.

Most important, I've learned that my uniquely beautiful life is an original work of art designed for my good and for the glory of the One who orchestrated my existence, even if it doesn't look like it at this moment. You are allowed to be both a masterpiece and a work in progress simultaneously.

> You are allowed to be both a masterpiece and a work in progress simultaneously.

Your life matters.

The girl of your dreams matters.

No matter how far you think you've drifted away from her, she's still there.

You, my friend, are a work of art. And your life can be beautiful.

As any artist will tell you, the key to creating a wonderful work of art is to be committed to the process. Beautiful creations take time. Sometimes they can be messy. And the artist often wrestles with how to produce a winning representation of what lives in the heart, mind, and soul.

The same is true for you. The key to living your beautiful life is to keep going. You must decide not to get hung up or stuck. Don't get bogged down in the mess that comes with making a masterpiece. Choose to wrestle for the win.

When I was a girl, I thought the choices would be easy, the decisions would be straightforward, and that life as I desired to live it would simply fall into my lap.

Choose to wrestle for the win.

Most of us already know that's not how life works.

Life is a series of experiences—some good, some not so good. Some parts we cruise through. Others we wrestle through as we attempt to get a grip on our stories. And let's be honest, we don't like to wrestle.

But often the winning is in the wrestling, and it's only as we continue to live that we see how all of those experiences fit together to make a complete picture.

You just have to keep going.

And believe in the idea of your masterpiece.

Is this my life?

That was my question as I was driving down the Dallas tollway and asking God to put a hurtin' on me.

And I've asked it over and over again.

Is this really my life?

Is this a question you've asked—or are asking—because your life isn't lining up with the hopes you harbored as girl, teenager, or young woman?

I hope so.

I hope that every now and again you stop to ask that question, and that when you do, you are willing to wrestle for the win if the answer is no.

I hope that you are willing to take note of every part of your story through the various seasons of life. Some parts will look like strokes of genius. Others may seem random, insignificant, or straight-up wrong.

Keep going.

Do the work.

Believe in the idea of a masterpiece. Ephesians 2:10 says, "For we are God's masterpiece. He has created us anew in Christ Jesus, so we can do the good things he planned for us long ago" (NLT).

The girl you wanted to be—or the girl you never were sure you could become—is already a divinely inspired masterpiece. Every day that you live, you have the opportunity to do the work of honoring the plan God has for you.

Maybe when you fell off of your track, you didn't ask God to break your legs. Maybe you're a little more stable than I was and didn't invite God to start an apocalypse in your life just because you were facing a difficult season. Or maybe your off-track seasons have been terribly worse.

Either way, I want you to know that you can get back on track.

And I want you to know that you have a friend.

I count it as my mission and privilege to share lessons learned from my journey so that you can know you are not the only girl who's felt lost in the middle of her life.

Is this your life?

Yes, yes, it is.

But this is me, your new friend, leaning in close with a smile to tell you this:

It's not too late to make it a life you love.

Reflections for the Rescue

REMEMBER

You are allowed to be both a masterpiece and a work in progress simultaneously.

REFLECT

- Have you ever had a "break my legs, God" moment? What did that moment teach you?
- Do you believe in the idea of a masterpiece for your life? Why or why not?
- What made you pick up this book? What is happening in your life that makes you want to hit the reset button?

RESPOND

You are a masterpiece. Write down three uniquely beautiful things about the girl in you.

Ephesians 2:10; Psalm 138:8; Psalm 143:5;
John 10:10; Jeremiah 29:11; Genesis 1:27–31.

FULL-BLOWN UGLY CRY

You Are Okay

O utside, I looked cool, calm, and collected.

Inside, I was experiencing a full-blown panic attack.

My husband and I sat on the same side of the table, facing the financial advisor and his assistant. We'd been married for fifteen years and had decided that now was a good time to get some professional direction in planning for our future.

Between that decision and the date of the appointment, my husband had lost his job. A loyal, hard worker, he had experienced many health challenges over the years and finally found himself no longer able to maintain the workload that had formed the foundation of our financial stability.

That meant it was now up to me.

As I sat there looking at the whiteboard where the financial advisor had carefully laid out a plan, all I saw was a big negative number. A negative number that I felt responsible for.

That moment was not the first time I'd been faced with hard circumstances, an insurmountable challenge, or a seemingly impossible situation.

Hard has an interesting way of finding me.

As a result, I've gotten good at pushing through things in my life. I logically think through what I can do to fix it, make it better, or rise above the storm.

But that doesn't mean I don't still feel the pressure.

The panic attack was controlled, tempered, and stuffed. I felt it threaten to rise up and make itself known in my face, in the tone of my voice, or in the words I used to communicate my thoughts.

And so I sat stoically in the financial advisor's office.

Serious.

Together.

Focused.

As a result of my effort to keep it together, I didn't have much to say. It was all so much to take in. The meeting concluded, and it was a long ride home.

The rest of the evening was normal. I was robotic, almost. Go home. Check. Fix dinner. Check. Read to kids, then pray with kids, then put kids to bed. Check. Quiet time for me. Check. Prepare to shut it down. Thank you, God, and check!

Movement.

Activity.

Routine.

I stayed in motion and kept to my routine so I wouldn't have to think about the problem that had presented itself to me earlier that afternoon.

And then the next morning came.

I went out for my morning run and found myself with no energy to keep the hard thoughts from coming. More than the run, I simply needed room to breathe.

And pray.

Lots and lots of prayer.

Huffing and puffing, I walked vigorously up the hill that begins where my driveway meets the rural road. My prayer began in those heavy breaths as I asked God what in the world He was doing and how He expected me to handle the hard that He'd so casually tossed my way. My questions quickly digressed into a rant of anger.

Anger at God.

I was angry because my life was hard and I had problems that seemed too heavy to carry with no end in sight.

Why me?

I never actually started running. Instead, I walked and wrestled with God for an hour.

As I returned to the edge of my driveway and prepared to re-enter the real world and get back to home, back to kids, and back to work, my phone rang.

My friend Shuna was on the line.

"Hey, girl! How ya doing?"

That was all it took.

My anger melted into an emotional flood.

I tried to fight it, but the previous day's strength and control had been squashed under the weight of the unknown.

The tears started, and they wouldn't stop. Everything that had been bottled up forced its way to the surface. Like lava flowing from a volcano, I cried uncontrollably—water poured out of my eyes, a wail escaped my lips, and I doubled over, powerless to stand up straight.

I entered a full-blown ugly cry. You know, the "Oprah cry."

Shuna waited, quietly offering a sensitive, "I'm so sorry!" "What's wrong?" or "Oh, no!" as I struggled to explain my plight while attempting to get myself together.

Reluctantly, I told her what had happened and how I felt. I told her I didn't think I could take one more step in this life that felt straight uphill. I huffed and puffed through staccato sentences, trying to explain my state of emotional and mental disarray.

She listened.

More important, she heard me.

And although she had no power to fix my problems, she did offer me something priceless, poignant, and precious.

"You are okay."

"You are going to be okay."

"It's going to be okay."

Shuna didn't offer a trite answer or a quick fix. There was no three-step plan or deep theoretical spiritual conversation.

She simply offered me hope.

And somehow, even though her words didn't magically erase my circumstances, they offered calm as a viable exchange for my crazy emotional rollercoaster ride.

Maybe you're facing your own kind of hard. Maybe thinking about it overwhelms you mentally or even overpowers you emotionally at times. Maybe you're a far cry from the you that you envisioned when you were a girl or the circumstances you dreamed would one day be your life. Maybe you didn't have extraordinary expectations, but even with low expectations, you're still deeply disappointed.

Your hard may not have anything to do with money. It may have to do with your marriage or your singleness. Your mental or physical health. You might be fighting addiction or paralyzing fear. Maybe you're worn out from mothering your kids or struggling with infertility.

Your hard might simply be that you can't figure out what comes next. Maybe you've arrived exactly where you aimed for and realized that where you worked so hard to get is not "the place" after all.

I want to offer you hope.

Where you are today is not where you have to be forever. You may not want to embrace where you are, but it is so incredibly important for you to embrace *who* you are. You get to choose. While you can't control everything in your life, you can do at least one thing: every day you get to choose to honor *you*.

There will never be another person who will grace the face of this earth who is like you.

There are people whom only you can love, places that only you can go, and things that only you can do the way that you would do them.

> You may not want to embrace where you are, but it is so incredibly important for you to embrace *who* you are.

You have the opportunity to choose every day to honor the loveliness that you uniquely bring to the world, even if the world doesn't seem to be holding up its end of the bargain to bring the lovely to you.

You are a unique creation. There is no one like you. And that is exactly what makes you so indescribably precious—and totally okay.

My first order of business on our journey together is to remind you that while you cannot control all of your circumstances, every day you can choose beliefs, attitudes, and actions that honor the best of who you are and who you can become.

Your belief will affect the attitudes you embrace and the lens through which you view your life. Your attitudes will steer your actions—what you say and what you do. What you say and do determines how you move from who you are today to who you will be tomorrow.

You get to choose.

If you choose to believe that you are defined only by your disappointments and disasters, you will abdicate your role in this world, the role that only you can play.

But if you choose to embrace your journey—even the parts that disappoint you, challenge you, or make you double over from the emotional weight of it all—you can one day look back and see your hard as a part of your life and not the definition of your life.

Shuna's offer of hope did not erase my hard; however, she did remind me that the way my life looks today is not the way it will look forever. She asked me to believe, and she reminded me that all I see is not all there is.

And I am asking you to believe.

Believe that your present is not all that is possible.

Believe that all you see is not all there is.

Today, my friend, this very moment, is just that, only a moment.

I want you to hold your head up and believe that where you find yourself right now—whether by mistake, choice, the impact of someone else's actions, unmet expectations, or even boredom—does not define you.

The mere fact that you are reading these words, breathing in and out, and therefore are alive indicates that you are worth the work of valuing who you are today and doing the work to discover who you can be tomorrow.

Believe that your present is not all that is possible.

In 1987, my family and I sat captivated like thousands of other people watching the attempt to rescue Jessica McClure. The eighteen-month-old girl had fallen twenty-two feet into a well and gotten lodged in a shaft only eight inches in diameter. We stayed glued to the television late into the night, then began watching CNN again early the next morning as we hoped and prayed with so many others that her life would not end in that well. We willed the equipment to open up a parallel path to her location and prayed for the strength of the workers who had not had any sleep in their effort to deliver the little girl back to her family.

For fifty-eight hours, the news channel kept people everywhere informed. The reporters told everyone watching how hard it would be to get to the little girl whose young and carefree life had been interrupted by this tragedy.

For much of the time that Baby Jessica was stuck underground, she let those within earshot know that she was alive. She "moaned, wailed and for a while even sang nursery rhymes to pass the time."[1]

As oxygen was pumped down the shaft to give her air, people kept calling to Baby Jessica, hoping for a response. Even though the situation was grim, her sweet little voice singing songs—along with her cries and moans—let everyone know that she was still there, alive, and worth the hard and diligent work of the rescue.

Years later, Jessica McClure has said she doesn't even remember that experience apart from what people have shared with her. Except for a scar on her forehead and a missing baby toe, Baby Jessica is just fine. She has gone on to live the life everyone hoped she would live.

Her darkest moment was only a moment in time.

Even though that little girl was once hurt, bruised, scared, and alone, her life is not some sad extension of that one event.

Jessica is still alive, and she is okay.

That memorable experience marked her life but did not define her life.

I've learned that is true for me, and I want you to know that is true for you as well.

Your life, my friend, does not have to be a sad sum total of your hard or your heavy.

Your darkest moments are only moments in time.

I would love to offer a simple answer or a quick fix, but here's the truth. Getting above ground can be hard work, and it can take some time.

Whether it's because of the dull ache of disappointment or the deep pain of some disaster or deep regret, you might feel as though the energy necessary to excavate yourself from the deep is . . .

Just.

Too.

Much.

But here's the bottom line, and I believe this with all of my heart:

You are worth the effort.

If you are breathing, you have life, and the life that has been given to you is a life that only you can live. You are the only person who can live your life with the unique combination of your gifts, talents, abilities, history, and design.

Don't give up, girl. You are worth the work of the rescue.

Fight for your life.

Every day. Get up. Keep going.

You are okay.

Come on, say it with me: "I am okay."

You may have to say this over and over again until you believe it, and if that's what it takes, do it.

Saying "I am okay" won't eliminate real problems or pressure, but it will allow you to offer yourself some hope. Your journey is a process, and it might take some time. Still, get up every day, look yourself in the mirror, and tell that girl inside you that she is okay.

You might have to get up with tears in your eyes, cries from your lips, or heaviness in your heart, but I want you to choose to believe your life is worth the effort.

> Your darkest moments are only moments in time.

Don't settle for staying stuck.

Decide to fight for your life.

And with God's help, choose attitudes and actions that will remind you of this:

You are okay.

You're still here. You're still alive. So you're still worth the work of the rescue.

Reflections for the Rescue

REMEMBER

Where you are today is not where you have to be forever.

REFLECT

- When was the last time you let out an ugly cry? What caused it?
- What difficulties are you facing that you feel buried underneath?
- Even if there is some darkness in your life right now, there is always light if you will just look for it. What is one thing in your life that is right?

RESPOND

Put this book down and look in a mirror. Go to your bathroom or pull a compact mirror out of your purse. Tell yourself you are okay and smile. Force the smile if you have to.

---

1 Timothy 6:12; Psalm 30:5; 2 Corinthians 4:17;
Romans 8:18; 1 Peter 1:6–7; Lamentations 3:21–24;
Psalm 34:17–18; Psalm 40:1–3.

GET OUT OF THE MIDDLE OF THE ROAD

Own Your Story

In my midtwenties, I took a business trip to San Francisco. I had been asked to go receive training for a new job (one that didn't make me want to ask God to break my legs). I'd never been to the city before and decided to stay an extra couple of days to see the sights.

During my stay I had the opportunity to bike across the Golden Gate Bridge, and to this day I count that experience as one of my favorite adventures of all time. My ride went exactly according to plan—a few miles along the coastline, a steep uphill climb to enter the path leading to the bridge, a cruise across the bridge overlooking the bay, and a smooth downhill sail to the quaint town of Sausalito, where I ate lunch, rested, and then headed back across the bay by ferry.

Perfect.

Almost a decade later, I decided to relive that San Francisco adventure, this time with my daughter and a girlfriend. I was, of course, excited about taking them to see the city I'd fallen in love with ten years before, but I was especially interested in introducing them to that fantastically flawless experience of biking across the bridge.

The morning after we arrived, we jumped on a trolley headed toward the waterfront to rent some bikes and begin our adventure. Leisurely riding through Fisherman's Wharf, past the marina, and through Presidio Park, we laughed and talked loud enough to hear each other over the noise of the ocean, seagulls, and nearby traffic. We pedaled toward the Golden Gate Bridge, stopping here and there for a photo before eventually dismounting our bikes to walk them up the steep hill to the mouth of the bridge. Then, with butterflies floating around in our tummies, we mounted the bikes, entered the pedestrians' path, and made our way across the famous landmark and over the San Francisco Bay. The day was beautiful, the views were perfect, and the three of us smiled with satisfaction as we took it all in.

After arriving at the other side and stopping for a few more pictures, we rode toward Sausalito. I was looking forward to the easy ride down that long slope into the quaint town.

About three minutes into the descent, I remember thinking that the bike was going too fast. And I remember thinking that I should probably brake just a bit to slow the bike down.

So I tapped on the brakes.

The bike stopped abruptly.

My body, on the other hand, did not.

I don't remember flying through the air. I don't remember hitting the pavement. I don't remember feeling any pain. I simply remember thinking, *Girl! Get yourself out of the middle of the road!*

As I crawled on my hands and knees to the shoulder of the road, I realized that my daughter had jumped off her bike and was crying and running toward me. My brain felt as if it were ricocheting back and forth inside my skull.

I felt a bit of an ache on my right side and a twinge of pain on my left, but those were not enough to distract me from my goal of getting to Sausalito. I figured I just needed a second—a chance to get my act together—and then we could be on our merry way.

I thought I would be okay.

My daughter didn't think so.

She asked me to look down at my shirt, and when I did, I realized it was covered with blood. I glanced at my left side to identify the source of the pain that was now radiating up my arm. My pinky finger was throbbing. It also seemed to be oddly shaped. I looked at my right arm and realized that my elbow was busted up.

My friend had called an ambulance, and when it arrived, one of the emergency medical personnel squatted in front of me, looking me over and asking me the types of questions you ask a girl who has just flown head-first off her bike.

"Are you okay?"

"Do you know your name?"

"Who's the president?

"What year is it?"

I guess the way I looked to the EMT, those questions were necessary. But I only felt irritated by his questions and offer of assistance. He was getting in my way.

All I wanted to do was get back on my bike and on my way to Sausalito.

Achiever. Control freak. Doggedly determined to make things work.

I reasoned with myself, figuring I could tolerate my pain long enough to get back on that bike and make it to Sausalito. Then I would put my bike on the ferry, pedal back across the bay to San Fran, and get myself to a hospital.

Insane. Crazy. *Muy estupido.*

The EMT closed his eyes and leaned his head to one side while taking a deep breath, willing himself to patience with this stubborn woman he had found himself caring for.

"You could, ma'am, but I don't recommend that. You are hurt, and I think you need to come with me so you can have your pain addressed."

I didn't want to admit that I needed help. I didn't want to acknowledge that my left pinky finger was hurting terribly (because it was broken), my right elbow was pulsing with pain (because it was fractured), and my brain was still ricocheting back and forth in my skull (because I had hit my head on the pavement). And I didn't want to confess that the sight of blood had totally unnerved me.

Never in a million years did I think I would take a trip designed for relaxation and pleasure only to find myself sitting on the side of the road injured.

All I'd wanted was another perfect day, another great experience, another adventure that lived up to my expectations.

Sometimes, though, our days don't live up to our expectations.

To find my way out of the mess I'd found my way into, I only had one option: I had to acknowledge my predicament.

I had to own my story in order to fix my story.

It takes one brave chick to admit that her life is not quite shaping up to be the life she envisioned. It takes courage to pause and assess your disappointment, realize where you've been disenchanted, and identify the source of your distress.

So many of us press through the pain without paying adequate attention to our brokenness. We disregard the ache in our hearts, as if ignoring the injury will cause the blood to stop flowing. We convince ourselves that somehow we don't need to deal with the distance between our expectations and our reality. We think that somehow, if we just keep going, the distance will simply close by itself.

It won't.

You and I must play an active role in closing that gap.

And the first step in closing the gap is to admit that the gap exists.

Step One is the highly familiar statement used in Alcoholics Anonymous (AA), an organization that helps people overcome an addiction to alcohol and to live sober. When someone shows up to an AA meeting and stands to speak, they begin by saying, "My name is 'So and So,' and I'm an alcoholic." People all over the world know and recognize that this first step in a series of twelve requires the struggling person to admit that he or she has a problem. In owning their story, they move one step closer to fixing it.

It's human nature to hide our shortcomings, disappointments, and mistakes. We don't like to be wrong, admit defeat, or show weakness. We tend to avoid the truth of our vulnerability, of our lack of control, of the pain of our predicament. We don't like others to know that we've messed up, that we don't feel capable, or that sometimes life just hurts.

But without confession, true restoration and healing cannot begin. If you really want help, you need to be willing to tell the truth to get it.

When you choose to own your story, you are not choosing to *wallow* in your mistakes, your pain, or your disappointments. You are simply choosing to be honest with yourself so that you can begin healing and move forward.

Okay, so here goes.

Step one.

Hello. My name is Chrystal, and I am an alcoholic.

> **Without confession, true restoration and healing cannot begin.**

Actually, that's not true. That's not my story.

But I *am* a girl who has struggled with insecurity, battled with promiscuity, experienced pregnancy outside of marriage, fought regularly with the #fatdemon, and wrestled with a sense of shame and insignificance because of it all.

You know.

Just to name a *few* things I've had to own.

Owning your story can be an uncomfortable first step, but in the words of Brene Brown, "Owning our story can be hard but not nearly as difficult as spending our lives running from it."[2] It might feel like you're coming out of hiding and seeing your scars for the first time in the full light of day. But telling yourself the truth is not an admission of powerlessness. It is when your story is in full view that you have the greatest ability to see what healing work needs to be done.

Owning your story is an act of strength.

You might be wondering if self-honesty must come solely from the less than stellar parts of your life. It doesn't have to. The key is full-out honesty in those areas where denial or half-truths prohibit you from moving forward. And often those areas are made up of less than stellar moments. This statement from Katherine Preston on the *Psychology Today* blog sums this idea up well: "There is no harm in speaking about the pieces of ourselves that we are proud of, and yet doing so does little more than inflate our own egos. The more powerful part of 'owning' our story is speaking about the pieces that make us feel embarrassed or ashamed. Bringing our greatest weaknesses out of the closet and into the spotlight."[3]

> Owning your story
> is an act of strength.

It doesn't matter how you got where you are as much as it matters that you acknowledge that where you are is not where you want to be.

When I went careening over the handlebars, it could have been because I was careless and tapped on the brakes too hard. Maybe I shouldn't have been moving that fast. It's also possible that the bike shop was to blame for sending me out on a bike with brakes pulled too tight. (I should have tried to sue 'em.) Or maybe it wasn't anyone's fault at all. Jacked-up stuff just happens sometimes.

It didn't really matter how I ended up on the side of the road. I simply needed to admit that sitting there broken and bruised was not where I wanted to be. I only needed to willingly receive the help being offered.

It doesn't really matter how I end up sidelined from the desired experience of my life. I simply need to admit that sitting there with a bleeding heart and a broken spirit is not where I want to stay and allow Someone who is offering aid to help me heal.

As a part of owning my story, I must also own that I'm a girl who has been raised in the church. I'm a preacher's kid. I know the Bible, and I've had a personal relationship with God for most of my life.

I was raised in a home where faith formed the core of our beliefs, gave a framework for our family, and provided a grid through which we interpreted and viewed our world. My siblings and I were all raised to believe that we were designed with a master plan in mind and that, as long as we loved God wholeheartedly, we would be able to tap into those plans and have the lives that He had especially designed for us to lead.

My mother made sure that I knew this verse in particular: "'For I know the plans I have for you,' declares the LORD, 'plans to prosper you and not to harm you, plans to give you hope and a future'" (Jer. 29:11). I grew up memorizing passages of Scripture that taught me my life could be abundantly full and overflowing (John 10:10 AMP).

You can imagine my surprise when I finally decided to own my story and then felt the impact of how far my life had veered from the plumb line of my expectations. The vision I'd been given for my life didn't match my actual life very much at all.

So I know what I'm talking about when I say that owning your story requires a bit of self-reckoning that isn't always easy.

But it all begins with telling the truth, truth that God already knows but wants us to be honest about for the benefit of our own healing. "For He knows the secrets of the heart" (Ps. 44:21).

Truth is always the best starting point of any journey forward. Psalm 51:6 says, "But you want complete honesty, so teach me true wisdom" (CEV). Wisdom for living the rest of your life begins with being honest about the life you have lived so far.

It takes courage to admit that

- things aren't working,
- parts of your life are disappointing,
- you've wasted time,
- you don't quite love the skin you are in,
- maybe you're a little bit unbalanced or even a little cray-cray.

(Don't worry about that last one. We all are just a tad.)

I know what I'm talking about when I say that it takes Someone outside of ourselves to reset what's broken, put what's been fractured back together, and give rest and restoration to quiet our minds, calm our hearts, and bring peace to our souls.

What about your story?

Maybe you didn't mean to end up on the other side of a broken relationship.

Maybe you've found yourself five, ten, or twenty years into a career that has gradually sucked the life out of you.

Maybe you've picked up a few extra pounds each year and, many years later, are waging a battle with your body that you just can't seem to win.

Maybe you've suddenly collided with the awareness that your dreams have gone unmet, and you're not sure you'll ever find that man, have that baby, or finish that degree.

Maybe you felt your life was beautiful until the unexpected call from the doctor, the unforeseen financial hardship, or the unanticipated emotional or mental crisis.

If I could sit down next to you when you are feeling the aches and pains that so often accompany reality, I'd look at you and tell you the truth.

Is this your life? Yes. Yes, it is.

Are you going to be okay? Yes. Yes, you are.

And as you slowly come to realize that what's bothering you needs more than just a bandaid, I'd encourage you to take the first step and own the narrative of your experience.

When you hurt, admit it.

When you feel pain, acknowledge it.

When you make mistakes, own up to them.

Your life does not have to be defined by the story you've lived thus far.

Be brave enough to believe you were made for more. Be bold enough to believe that healing can take place and that change is possible. And change is *always* possible. Even if your circumstances can't change, your attitude toward them can.

> Be brave enough to believe you were made for more.

Dare to trust that it's God's desire for you to live out a beautiful story designed with you in mind.

Choose to take Step One.

Choose to own your story.

Be honest.

Tell the truth.

The good, the bad, and the ugly. Whatever happened, you survived. You are still here.

Own your story.

The girl you want to be is depending on you.

Reflections for the Rescue

REMEMBER

Owning your story is an act of strength.

REFLECT

- Are you comfortable owning your story? Why or why not?
- Is your life measuring up to your expectations? Why or why not?
- In what ways have you been hurt or disappointed? Have you healed from those hurts and disappointments? Why or why not?

RESPOND

Take time to heal. As you continue to read, own your story. Over the next seven days, spend a few minutes each day writing down defining moments in your life's story.

2 Corinthians 12:9; Psalm 15:1–2; John 8:32;
Jeremiah 12:3; Psalm 139:1; Psalm 145:18.

GOOD GIRL . . . HIS GIRL

A Chapter from My Story

Peple always want to know how a girl who has a great family, a great upbringing, and what seems to be a great future can end up making not so great choices. It always seems to surprise people when the preacher's kid makes a mistake, has a struggle, or misses the mark.

Well, let me tell you. It might surprise the preacher's kid too.

I was smart. A straight-A student and usually the teacher's pet. As a teenager, I was a "good girl" by all standards, and I liked it that way. I was proud to know that I pleased my parents and myself by doing things well. I was also very involved in my church youth group. I participated in most of the opportunities to gather, serve, and hang out. I was a leader. I got things done. So apart from being the pastor's oldest daughter, I also stayed visible because I was always running something.

Focused. In charge. Maybe a bit bossy at times. I knew what was important, and I ran hard after those things.

There is no way I would have believed you if at that time you'd told me what my life would be like just a few years later. I was too sure, too confident, too on top of things. And this is exactly why the unfamiliar surprises. It creeps up. Change happens gradually. We don't see it coming. One day we simply look up and are surprised that we no longer recognize the person we've become or the life we are living.

How do I know this?

Because it happened to me.

Imagine you are joining me on my front porch to sip hot chocolate or something else warm and soothing. It's late in the evening, maybe even close to midnight, because that's when girls talk and share all their secrets. I want to share a chapter from my story with you.

If I'm telling you to be brave enough to tell the truth, it's only right that I go first.

I remember the first time he held my hand.

We were in a little house that my church had converted into a youth center. We gathered there every Wednesday night with other teenage kids to study God's Word, sing songs, and have fun and fellowship.

I'd heard that he liked me, but I wasn't really that interested. Mainly because I wasn't that interested in boys. I was much more interested in making the most of my life and trying to discern, even at a young age, how I wanted to live it.

But I do remember when he held my hand.

It was time to close our time of Bible study with prayer, and, just so that he could hold my hand, he crossed the room.

I was an embarrassed fifteen-year-old girl who was being forced, in front of a room filled with her peers, to acknowledge that there was a boy who liked her and wanted everyone else in the room to know.

That first time was not the last. He made it his business to cross the room and hold my hand every single time we closed in prayer. It became somewhat of a joke, something that was expected.

Week after week, teenagers around the room laughed and giggled while I bit my bottom lip out of embarrassment. It was obvious that I loathed the unsolicited attention.

But I was the nice girl.

I didn't want to be mean, and I didn't want him to feel rejected. I figured that I would have to hold somebody's hand anyway, so why not his?

This went on for months—actually, the better part of a year. Then one day, he didn't cross the room.

This weekly action had come to be something that I, as well as everyone else, had come to expect, and the absence of his movement was silently deafening.

Over time, something had changed. I'd gotten accustomed to this boy's attention. As he consistently expressed his desire to show me that he cared, I gradually let down my guard. The laser beam focus on my own life, goals, and dreams slowly blurred into the starry-eyed gaze of a teenage girl's what-ifs, maybes, and could-happens.

So the day he chose not to cross the room, I felt a void.

I remember thinking that maybe I ought to give him a chance. I remember thinking that maybe he wasn't as much of an interruption as I'd thought. I remember thinking that he wasn't all that bad and that being good friends probably wouldn't do much to interrupt my life.

But the day he stopped holding my hand was the day I started to drift. It was the beginning of drifting out of my own lane and into another.

I got distracted.

Motivated and preoccupied by a heightened sense of significance and blinded by the excitement of something different and new, the pursued became the pursuer.

Polite chance interactions became more purposeful as I initiated conversation to let him know there was an interest on my part. I lingered a little longer. Asked more questions. Provided fuller answers. I was truly happy to be his friend, the kind of friend who hopes for more than friendship.

As time went on, our friendship grew and I wanted more. More of the feelings, more of the attention, more of him. Where my energy had previously been focused on what mattered to me for my future, it morphed into a focus on what mattered to me right now. And he was what mattered.

The girl I had been faded into the shadows, bit by bit, day by day.

The thing is, the change in my head and in my heart happened slowly. I didn't notice it. My mindset, actions, and attitudes shifted incrementally over time. Little by little, the distraction and excitement of young love threw me off my game, and I lost sight of the girl I'd been committed to becoming.

But I didn't realize it.

I slowly morphed from a self-confident, goal-oriented young woman who had a healthy expectation about her potential into a girl who was desperate for the attention and affection that she'd become accustomed to receiving. Little by little I grew more and more attached to this young man who made me laugh and seemed to hold me in high esteem.

Schoolwork got less of my time. My grades slipped. I cared less about being the good girl and more about being *his* girl. Pleasing my parents became secondary to spending time with him, talking to him, and feeling those butterflies of first love. I was less of a leader and more of a bystander. Taking on responsibility of any kind wasn't as fun because it meant I would spend less time hanging with him. The intentional and direction-oriented choices of a driven, motivated teenage girl were reduced to unintentional and involuntary reactions. I lost control as my visibility decreased and the relationship obscured everything.

Even when my parents, youth leaders, or even friends questioned me about my change in behavior, attitude, and involvement, I failed to notice any cause for concern. Nor did I really care. At that point, I can't say I was really listening to the questions, opinions, or concerns of others. How could I hear them when I couldn't even hear the voice of the girl inside? I had all but silenced the very one whose life I'd been so focused on before.

And if that girl was trying to get my attention, I'd drifted too far away from her to hear her clearly.

———⌒———

Drifts in life don't last forever. Unintentional living eventually reaches a dead end, and to move in any direction requires a decision or a turn.

As young love often does, something delightful and innocent quickly descended into an emotional and physical rollercoaster ride. I'd become addicted to the young man's approval, overtures, and acceptance. He'd grown accustomed to the reality that I was willing to abdicate my own worth to obtain his affection.

You could say I was drunk in love.

And like anyone desperate for that which they have cultivated a craving, I was willing to do whatever it took to get it.

> **Drifts in life don't last forever. Unintentional living eventually reaches a dead end.**

Right ways of thinking, right choices, and right behaviors, once clear-cut and obvious, now seemed to be relative and optional. Bottom line? I did whatever I felt like doing.

I was no longer drifting. I was making decisions. Poor decisions, to be more specific.

Decisions to disobey my parents and the rules they had set up for my protection.

Choices to ignore the wisdom I'd been taught about protecting and respecting my heart, my mind, and my body.

Actions that did not align with what I believed.

I followed fast the road that led to what I thought I wanted. I remember sensing the need to slow things down, to be more cautious, and to think more clearly about the direction in which I was headed, but it's hard to stop something moving at breakneck speed. It's a challenge to react appropriately when your senses and sensibilities are impaired.

Fast bikes moving down steep hills often don't have pretty endings.

The farther I went, the more numb I became to the voice of the girl within who was trying to get my attention and tell me I was headed the wrong way. A vicious cycle repeated in my head and in my heart. The more I silenced, ignored, or debated with the girl inside, the smaller she got and the less I noticed her. Guilt, shame, and self-condemnation grew to fill the place she left void.

I learned to function from an insecure place. I learned to pretend that the life I was living was the life I wanted.

It wasn't.

But I was too busy being in love to notice.

Before my senior year in high school started, I was no longer a virgin. The relationship that had started between two young people in a church youth group with the most innocent of intentions had turned into a full-out disaster.

It all happened so fast. I hadn't noticed how much I'd gradually shifted away from the strong, determined girl I'd once been. I'd lowered the high standards I'd fiercely held, released many expectations of my life, and no longer cultivated the faith that had sustained me.

My drift had led me far away from the girl I'd planned on being in this season of my life. My decisions carried me quickly along in a raging current far beyond my control.

Don't worry, I won't leave you hanging. I'll get back to my story in a little while. But first I need you to understand something that will help you in your story.

Sometimes we drift.

Drifts happen when we unintentionally move away from who we believe we can be, what we believe we can accomplish, or where we hope our lives will take us. A drift is "the decision you make by not deciding."[4]

While the details I've shared with you about one of my own drifts (yes, there have been others) is primarily centered around the emotional pull of a girl who craved the attention and affection of a boy, drifts come in all shapes and sizes. Think about your own drifts. The trip through your own narrative is a trip worth making.

Maybe, like me, you've lost focus because of the pull of a relationship that derailed your intentions, plans, or purposes. But maybe not. Drifts are not solely romantic ones, nor are all drifts related to morality. Maybe the drift in your life came because you simply got tired of trying.

Maybe you reached a point where you simply got tired of doing the work of living purposely, steering and pushing your way forward. It could be that you only meant

> The trip through your own narrative is a trip worth making.

to take a break, but by the time you took notice, the break had gone on for years, leaving you far from the person you'd wanted to be or the plans you'd had.

Maybe you took a break from school, but haven't yet gone back. Maybe you had a financial goal but got tired of the sacrifice, so you relaxed your spending habits, stopped saving, and no longer kept that detailed spending review. Maybe you were doing well on your weight-loss journey, but one special occasion—strung together with just a few more—set you on a long-term path that led you more than a few pounds back up the scale. Those cupcakes will kill ya.

Maybe your drift happened when you were a teenager—young, easily influenced, and unprepared for the determination it takes to stay on course. Or maybe until now, everything in your life has gone as planned, but after climbing the career ladder, getting married and having kids, or finishing that advanced degree, you just aren't sure what comes next. So you wander, aimlessly marking time, not exactly sure where to go from here.

Maybe you drifted because you were busy doing the immediate, the urgent, and the unignorable—changing diapers as a stay-at-home mom, keeping the peace between family members, or working two and a half jobs to keep things afloat. Then, somewhere, in the process of doing all that needed to be done, you drifted away from *you*.

When you realize how far you've drifted and how far away you are from the life you hoped for, it certainly can be overwhelming. But there is always an anatomy to our drifts. We didn't meander miles away in a minute. Slowly and gradually we took steps, possibly unconsciously, that took us farther than we intended. However, if we pause to examine our drifts and see them for what they are—small abdications over time—we realize that we do indeed have the power to change. We can know that our drift is not as big, overpowering, or insurmountable as it seems.

Here's the good news. If there is a way in, there is a way out. While you may feel utterly lost, take comfort in this: lost does not equal lifeless.

> **Lost does not equal lifeless.**

And as long as there is still life, there is hope.

Hope for getting back on track.

Hope for finding your way.

Hope for the girl who is still there.

Reflections for the Rescue

REMEMBER

The trip through your own narrative is a trip worth making.

REFLECT

- After hearing some of my story, identify at least one drift in your life. What role did your feelings play in your drifting experience?
- When did this drift happen? Why did it occur?
- Are you in a drift? If you aren't sure, ask a friend.

RESPOND

Take the next step. Be brave enough to be vulnerable. Share a chapter from your story with a trusted friend. If you are not ready for this level of honesty, simply tell a friend that you are working on owning your story—drifts and all. Ask them to pray for you as you do.

James 1:12–16; Hebrews 2:1; Proverbs 4:23;
1 Peter 2:10–11; 1 John 1:6.

HERSHEY AND THE HIGHWAY

The Anatomy of a Drift

I was on a long drive—a three-hour drive, to be exact—headed from one Texas town to another.

I'd filled my car full of gas and my purse with a few snacks to make sure that I could complete the trip without stopping to put fuel in my car or my tummy.

The best snack in my purse? Hershey bar with almonds.

That was the one I was saving for just the perfect moment.

When that time came, I reached into my purse and felt around for it, combing every nook and cranny of my bag with the tips of my fingers, expecting at any moment to feel the smooth wrapper underscored by the bumpy goodness held inside.

The bar wasn't in there.

I looked over to the passenger seat and then to the floor below.

There it was.

My Hershey bar was on the floor. Somehow it had fallen out of my purse.

Vexed about the dilemma of the snack being just out of my reach,

I could hardly focus on the road. My brain went into overdrive trying to figure out how to get to my chocolate without having to stop the car.

I felt the etchings of the freeway underneath my tires.

That chocolate bar was distracting me.

And my distraction caused me to drift ever so slightly outside the safety of the yellow lines.

Drifts happen because we get distracted. We might be preoccupied by something that isn't good for us, or we might be preoccupied with doing the next thing. For a moment—or in a series of moments—we don't pay close attention to who we are. We cease focusing intently on who we want to be, or maybe we never even started. We lose awareness, or maybe we never knew that living with awareness is important. We acquiesce to whatever comes next, inattentive to the cost of our lack of participation. We're too busy living to notice we're meandering away from a meaningful path, despite our best intentions.

Many of us live distracted because we live busy. Maria Popova, in her weekly literature review, *Brain Pickings*, says, "I frequently worry that ... busyness [is] the greatest distraction from living, as we coast through our lives day after day, showing up for our obligations but being absent from our selves, mistaking the doing for the being."[5]

Distractions can seem so much more exciting than the rhythm of the everyday, the boredom of the expected, or the ongoing discipline to accomplish something worthwhile. But while distractions might seem to give you life, the reality is that they can steal your life.

Distractions will tempt you to avert your eyes from the path you believe is right or the destination you hope is yours as you gaze at something that is shiny, interesting, different, entertaining, or amusing. That first peek may not be problematic, but as anyone who has stared too long at a billboard can tell you, where your eyes go, your car can easily follow.

How do you stay on track or get back on track in your life? The same way you stay on the road when you are behind the wheel.

The antidote for distraction is focus—the choice to pay attention and live aware.

⁓

I drove a little farther, jolted to attention by the reminder from the road to stay in my lane.

It wasn't long, however, before I started thinking about that Hershey bar again.

But now, instead of simply being distracted by it, I tried to convince myself that I could reach over and grab it without consequence.

As much as I knew deep down that this action could be detrimental, I wanted what I wanted and started strategizing how I could get it without incident. I moved quickly from distracted thoughts to deceptive thoughts, the kind of thoughts that happen when we don't want to admit that there are consequences for our actions.

> The antidote for distraction is focus—the choice to pay attention and live aware.

Drifts continue when we deceive ourselves into thinking things aren't that bad. We drift when we rationalize away the truth and deceive ourselves. After distraction has carried us a little way, our conscience might try to call us back to being sensible. We might even have friends, family, or acquaintances ask us about the changes they've noticed in our actions or attitudes, but we tell ourselves and others that we're not really that far off course. We are convinced that what others notice isn't really that terrible or isn't that out of character. And so we justify. Defend. Vindicate. Or attempt to explain away.

Deception occurs when we've grown accustomed to the distraction. In order to continue in what was once uncomfortable, we develop a level of comfort. We learn to justify what was once unreasonable. We choose to ignore the facts of the important for the feeling of the insignificant.

The only way to fight deception is to face the truth head on.

But what happens if you don't?

After a while, I'd rationalized away any thought that opposed reaching for that candy bar. I no longer heard the voice of reason. I no longer felt the fear of taking the chance. I no longer saw the problem with taking a few seconds to grab the goodness sitting on the floor of the passenger seat.

I was consumed with the right now, the immediate.

While my conscience had tried to warn me, I was no longer bothered by thoughts of danger, lack of safety, or even the accidental loss of my life. I worked hard at discrediting the voice of reason. I no longer listened. I chose not to respond.

Distraction and deception had worn down my sensitivities.

Drifts persist because we become desensitized. Once we've gone too far, too long, we become less shocked by and less sensitive to the changes that we have allowed. The "every once in a while" becomes our norm. We no longer have an inner argument each time we move farther away from our best self—that girl within us and everything she hopes to be. The change that might at one time have made us uncomfortable, now seems commonplace. We become numb to things we once would have had a strong reaction to. We don't notice the problem anymore, so we don't engage. We've forgotten we were ever on a path at all. Most terrible, we might adopt a cynicism toward all we'd hoped before because we've stopped believing in who we were and the dreams we'd had.

And when that girl calls, when the one we hoped we could be beckons us, we don't listen or respond because we don't think she knows what she's talking about. We don't trust her. Sometimes we've drifted so far that we don't hear her calling at all. But the only way you can respond to your life is by choosing to listen to your life. Yes, you might feel discomfort, but then you can decide to do something about it.

Let me pause to say that some of you may think I'm blowing all of this out of proportion. You may recognize a small drift of some kind in your life but don't agree that being off course a tad can affect the trajectory of your life. Even small drifts matter. In the words of Mary Kay Ash, "Some people drift through their entire life. They do it one day at a time, one week at a time, one month at a time. It happens so gradually they are unaware of how their lives are slipping away until it's too late." Please consider the "one in sixty" rule of navigation. For every degree you are off in your direction now, you will be approximately one mile off sixty miles later.

> **A small drift left unattended will, over time, make a huge impact on your final destination.**

A small drift left unattended will, over time, make a huge impact on your final destination.

I decided to reach for the Hershey bar.

I took my eyes off the road for just a few seconds, leaned way over to the right, and stretched my arm as far as it would go.

For a moment, I felt the victory of holding the chocolate bar in my hands. The victory was short-lived, though, because I almost simultaneously felt the etchings of the freeway underneath my tires again.

But this time the etchings weren't a warning. They were an indication that I was losing control and flying off the freeway. Shortly after, I felt the rumble of uneven ground as the car careened over grass, rocks, and dirt.

Drifts and decisions play a central role in the direction of our lives. While a drift occurs through no clear choice of your own or of someone else's, a decision marks a moment when you participated in picking the route.

Sometimes your decisions are made flippantly. You may choose without truly counting the cost or understanding the impact your choice will have in the next year or ten years.

Maybe your decision to move across country for the promotion was not a bad one, but you didn't account for the loneliness you'd encounter being away from your family and friends. Maybe deciding to go to the college of your dreams seemed perfectly fine when you received your acceptance letter, but years later you are disgusted with the amount of debt you are in. Or maybe you love your children and can't imagine life without them, but you had no clue how much they would cost, how much of yourself you'd have to give, or how much they would break your heart when they became adults.

Just like drifts, decisions can result in lots of justification and have a numbing effect where you disassociate yourself from your choices. You might blame others for the decisions you "had" to make, or take on a victim's mentality—a mindset that says you are not responsible for your actions.

The good news is that if you are in a drift or are dealing with the result of a decision, there is a remedy. No matter how far or how long you've drifted or how many decisions you've made that turned you around and left you clueless as to how to get back, there is an antidote.

You, my dear, have the ability to choose.

I sat in the median, stunned.

Let's be honest, I felt like a total idiot.

I mean, who puts their life at risk for a chocolate bar? Apparently me, that's who.

I gathered my wits and realized that the situation could have been much worse. The car could have flipped, hit a tree, or gone flying across the median and into the lanes of oncoming traffic.

My car had shut off, so I turned the key in the ignition to see if it would start and breathed a sigh of relief when it did. There was still power. I had another chance.

A chance to drive with care and get to my intended destination.

I drove out of the dip in the median and slowly merged back onto the Texas highway. With my Hershey bar in hand, I vowed that I would never be so careless behind that wheel.

More important, upon arriving in one piece, I thanked God for His protection, and resolved that in the future, I would always secure my snacks safely within my reach.

The drift didn't have to happen. I had a choice.

My friend, you can choose to live aware, to acknowledge the truth, and to listen to the story of the life that is yours and yours alone. You have the power to change your course. You can either take action or you can determine your reaction to the story that has unfolded thus far.

> **You, my dear, have the ability to choose.**

If you have a sense of discomfort about your life, that is a gift. Your discomfort is a signal that something needs to change. It is the call of the girl inside asking you not to give up and to fight for her. The mere fact that you have a sense of dis-ease about your life is a testament to the fact that you know deep down you were made for more.

Can I tell you that you were indeed made for more?

And it doesn't matter if you've drifted a little or if you are smack dab in the middle of a ditch. No matter where you are or what you've been through, you still have power. The girl in you still has a chance.

Reflections for the Rescue

REMEMBER

You, my dear, have the ability to choose.

REFLECT

- What are some distractions that are preventing you from living fully aware?
- How have you rationalized staying in a drift?
- Are you desensitized? What used to bother you that you no longer notice?
- What decisions have you made that have resulted in consequences you are living with now?

RESPOND

Write this affirmation down somewhere where you will see it and see it often:

I'm still here. God's not finished with me yet.

Philippians 3:13–14; 1 Peter 3:10–11; Isaiah 30:15;
Luke 5:31–32; 2 Corinthians 7:9–10.

PART 2

LOOK AT YOUR LIFE

Too many people overvalue what they are
not and undervalue what they are.
—*Malcolm S. Forbes*

God made no mistakes when He
created you. You were uniquely designed
for success in your purpose.
—*Valorie Burton*

AN EPISODE FROM ADOLESCENCE

You Are a Soul

I was twelve.

I don't recall whether I'd started my period, but one thing was for sure, I was totally hormonal.

Searching frantically to make sense of a world that was changing by the millisecond, I found my emotions riding the waves of adolescence and not holding up too well. My young mind and heart had jumped on a rollercoaster ride without my approval, and I didn't have a strong stomach. I was throwing up attitude, anger, and anxiety everywhere.

This evening was no different.

What the impetus of this particular day's volatile explosion was, I know not. I simply remember the eruption. I sat in my room alone, tears running hot and heavy down my face, heaving deeply as my heart beat hard inside my chest. My emotions were palpable. And I decided I simply couldn't take it any longer.

Walking with passion down the hallway, I made the short trip from the room I shared with my sister to my parents' bedroom door and knocked firm and heavy. Not waiting for the answer, I turned the knob and stepped inside their room.

My mother was beginning to unwind and unwrap from the workday's attire, accessories, and accouterments. Her heels were off, one earring had found its way to the dressing table, and as she turned her eyes to acknowledge my arrival, her hands were poised to remove the other. My father had unbuttoned his shirt enough to breathe a bit. His tie lay across the end of the bed, and he padded across the floor in those black stripe-stitched socks that men wear when they go to work in suits.

For a moment, I hesitated. I wanted to hide. I wanted to turn around and go back down the hallway, where I could jump into my bed, bury my head in my pillow, and soak the pillowcase with a flood of tears.

But instead, I chose to share my outburst, because that's how twelve-year-old girls roll. I took a deep breath and then filled the air with a heartrending, guttural cry.

"I don't know who I am!"

Silence.

My mother's hand was still poised to remove her earring. My father stopped midway across the room and stared at me blankly.

"What?" he said.

"I don't know who I am!" I repeated with a little less force.

The explosion had already happened. Now I was just left with a minor burst of lava, but the majority had already spewed forth and was now flowing through the minds of my parents as they processed my statement.

"What do you mean you don't know who you are?" My mother still had one hand on that earring.

"I don't know. I just know I don't know who I am!"

The truth is that my oversimplified statement attempted to express, in six words, what many people spend weeks, months, or even years trying to dissect, examine, and rhetorically share in a healthy way.

But I was twelve and in a full-blown identity crisis. I teetered on the edge of a crucial search for self, significance, and purpose—a journey of self-discovery that, for some, can last a lifetime.

The question I posed to my parents that night—the question asked in my fit of "tweeny-bopper" emotion—still cannot be answered in a simple sentence.

In fact, that question has repeated itself at other moments in my life.

Thirty years later, I've realized that many people don't know how to answer it.

When asked who they are, many will respond with what they do, whom they have relationships with, or what they have experienced or achieved.

The problem is these things can all change.

The problem can also be that *we* change.

Without a proper sense of identity, we will drift and turn. Our feelings can ebb and flow based on our circumstances. Our sense of self can bend or break based on the opinions, words, or actions of others. And things only get more complicated when a crisis hits.

The very idea of a drift is based on the assumption that there is a place we're supposed to be. It assumes that we're drifting away from something—or someone.

So here's the question we must answer if we are truly going to honor the person we were designed to be: That girl inside you, where should she be and what should she be doing?

And the next question: How do you figure this out?

Honey, let me just stop here real quick and set the record straight. We're *all* trying to figure it out. Even if you think you have it all together, in one moment life can shift on you, presenting the need to rebalance, refocus, and reaffirm what you believe about the girl you truly are.

Knowing who you are is crucial, but it is also a process. Self-understanding, self-appreciation, and self-love are things you can build over time as you give yourself the grace to learn what makes you "you" and see the unique beauty you can bring to the world.

Out of all the things I share with you in this book that will help you stop the drift, this is the most important.

You have to believe in who you are.

And if you don't know who you are, you must choose to value the "gift of you" enough to begin discovering who you truly are.

Here's a great starting place for seeing yourself in a new way: *you are a uniquely and divinely created soul, designed to be filled by a living Spirit that is housed inside of a physical body.* We live in a world that seeks to convince us otherwise. More than ever before, we're bombarded with messages that we are creatures of chance who have no purpose or plan apart from whatever we might happen to figure out on our own. This point of view is relentlessly promulgated in education, in the media, and even in conversations at the water cooler that seek to strip humanity of the fact that we are special. We are creatures who have a natural propensity toward spiritual things because we are spiritual beings.

You are a soul. You are not a product of random forces that ordered themselves miraculously into the exact arrangement necessary to produce life. You are more than the 37.2 trillion cells that comprise what you see when you look in the mirror.[6] You are more than your hair color, the elasticity of your skin, or the shape of your derriere. You exist beyond the physical. You are an invisible, immaterial essence that is more marvelously complex than anyone will ever know. While you are closely tied to your physical experience, you extend beyond the physical limitations of the body you are in and of the planet you call home. No matter what reflection stares back at you or what frame you see in family photos, the real you will always lie just behind the twinkle in your eye.

You are created. Who and what you are is determined by the one who made you and brought you into existence. You are not left alone to figure out what to do with the one life you've been given to live. You are a divinely inspired work of art. You are made in the image of a living God who didn't dump you on the planet to spend a lifetime lost and with no clue how to exist well and have days that matter for more.

Believing this fully and completely matters. You have more at stake than a rock on the side of the road or a flower that blooms in a garden or a tree that grows in the forest. When God said, "Let Us make man in Our image, according to Our likeness" (Gen. 1:26 NASB), He gave you priority over other living creatures and forms of life. You were designed for more.

You are unique. Your purpose was built into your packaging. When God created you, He made you totally different from any other human being who has lived or will ever live on this earth. Your fingerprints are distinct. Your DNA is not repeated in any other human being. Your "deoxyribonucleic acid, as it is rarely pronounced, is the genetic formula that tells your cells how to build you into you, and no one else."[7] The patterns of your iris differ in each eye; this is true even in identical twins. You have distinct patterns of blood vessels displayed on your retinas that provide a precise unrepeatable snapshot of your nervous system.

You are a divinely inspired work of art.

Everything about your design says that there is no one like you.

Your soul is the essential, immaterial element of your being. From it you possess a sense of identity based on your personality, emotional makeup, thoughts, and actions.

You are not an accident or an afterthought. You are here and conscious of your existence because Someone had you particularly and purposely in mind when you were given the gift of life.

You don't *have* a soul; you *are* a soul—a uniquely and divinely created one at that.

When I told my parents in a fit of teenage confusion that I had no idea who I was, I was not considering my special design and the truth that the combination of everything that makes me "me" was something to cherish, to study, to understand, and to celebrate.

My feelings—and hormones—were overruling the fact that I was a fantastic female, rare in creation and never to be repeated again.

And so are you.

Most women I know struggle, at some point in their lives, to keep that special design in mind. We get ditched by the boy, stressed by our finances, fired from the job, snubbed by our kids, bored with our life, disgusted by our weight gain, ashamed of our wrinkles, and are left wondering if we actually matter. When you understand that you are a diamond mine of a physical, emotional, and mental combination that has come together in a one-of-a-kind way, that knowledge can change what you see when you look in the mirror.

You are not an accident or an afterthought.

As my tweenage self stood looking at my parents and waited to hear their well-thought-out response, my dad stared intently at me, his eyes full of disbelief and confusion.

And then he laughed.

And then he laughed a little harder.

Once he started, it was as if he didn't have the power to stop.

And I lie not when I tell you that this story is still one that will occasionally surface during family get-togethers, and my dad laughs just as hard now as he did then.

He laughed because he thought it was comical how difficult I was making a seemingly simple matter.

"What do you mean? You are *Chrystal*!"

His answer was not satisfactory.

"But who is Chrystal?" I asked.

"Oh, my *goodness*."

"I'm serious, Daddy!"

But I couldn't help allowing a slight smile to break through the tears that had just a few seconds before streamed down my face.

"You are Chrystal!" he said with a smile of compassion and understanding. "That's all you need to know."

My crisis of identity was deeply felt but apparently also surprisingly uncomplicated.

I was Chrystal—and a uniquely and divinely created one at that. For that moment, this was all I needed to know, appreciate, and accept.

Since that adolescent episode, I've learned a lot about myself. I've learned what I like and dislike. I've learned what I'm good at and what tasks I should never be given. I'm learning every day how to better take note of and appreciate the landscape of my life. I can tell you what in my life is beautiful to behold and what places will remain dry and barren if I don't water them well. I've lived long enough to know more but not to know all.

Most important, I've learned to love the process of appreciating and honoring my soul.

Knowing what makes you "you" is a process. The art of communicating that both to yourself and to the world around you can take time to develop, hone, and fine-tune.

It's not so much about *having* the answer as it is about learning the answer. It's not so much about delivering a well-rehearsed response as it is about the process of learning the landscape of your life and understanding what is truly there, what needs to be refined, and what is beautiful just as it is in the raw.

> It's not so much about *having* the answer as it is about learning the answer.

But what if raw is not very beautiful at all right now?

What if your life is falling apart? What if you can't find the energy to hope for better because all of your energy is being spent on each breath you take? What if the pain of what life has sent your way or what you have invited in is now too great to bear and you are simply surviving—bare of hope, bereft of dreams, and lacking any vision?

I know how you feel. I've been there.

Which is why I know that you are in just the right place to begin the wonderful process of self-discovery.

Begin with the decision to value your soul, but also accept that knowing who you are is a lifelong process and a labor of love.

Be patient with yourself. It takes time to rebalance, refocus, and reaffirm what you believe about the girl in you. Know, appreciate, and accept what you know today, and look forward to what you will learn tomorrow.

But if all you have today is your name and a statement of belief that you are remarkably uncommon and incredibly distinct, that's all you need to know.

Reflections for the Rescue

REMEMBER

You don't *have* a soul; you *are* a soul—a uniquely and divinely created one at that.

REFLECT

- How have you been tempted to devalue the uniqueness of your soul?
- What keeps you from believing in your value?
- Do you struggle with being patient with yourself? Why or why not?

RESPOND

Write your name in the blank below:

I am _____, and I'm a uniquely and divinely created soul.

Now write that statement somewhere you will see it often. Write it on your mirror with a dry-erase marker or lipstick. Jot it on a three-by-five card and keep it taped on the dashboard of your car.

Genesis 2:7; 1 Thessalonians 5:23;
Jeremiah 1:5; Psalm 139:13–14; 2 Corinthians 4:16;
Psalm 62:1; Isaiah 43:1.

CHAPTER 7

DOUBLE BLUE LINES

Chronicle of a Collision

Walking down the sidewalk on the college campus, I felt nothing. Numb.

Void of pain or pressure.

Empty.

Stunned.

Pregnant.

I tried to accept the raw reality of my unexpected situation, but I just couldn't bring myself to do it. I'd started out so well. I'd had a plan and a vision for what I thought I would do with my life, but somewhere along the way I'd lost clarity and focus. That vision of who I was and what I thought could come of my life blurred into an unrecognizable mess.

But I had just seen blue double lines in full twenty-twenty.

There was no mistaking that the pregnancy test was positive. But that didn't stop me from taking a couple more tests. You know, just to be sure.

Nineteen years old. Second semester of my freshman year in college.

My drifts and decisions had turned into a head-on collision.

My knee-jerk reaction was to share my shocking news with the young man I was sure would help me figure out what to do next. We had been high school sweethearts. His athletic scholarship and my academic scholarship had placed us on the same college campus. He was just a short distance away.

I had the pregnancy test in my coat pocket. I didn't know how to tell him. I figured physical evidence would do the trick.

I knew he would be in study hall, so I went and asked him to come to a spot where we could have more privacy.

I pulled the pee stick out of my pocket.

We both just stared at it.

And then came those words that no girl ever wants to hear.

"It's not mine."

Crash.

Impact.

Collision.

I stood there with a blank look and an open mouth. What he was suggesting wasn't even possible.

Then came the feeling of pain, a sensation of pressure, and a flood of thoughts that were fighting each other to become words I could speak out loud.

None came.

But the tears did.

I turned and walked out of the building, feeling the gut-wrenching pain of total rejection. The fear of an unknown future. And the anxiety that accompanies knowing you are totally lost, in the dark, with no clue how to find your way.

The tears forced their way out of my body, hot, fast, and furious. They flowed and continued to flow like a leaky faucet for days, weeks, and months.

I can't tell you how many times during those difficult days I wondered how I'd ended up pregnant and alone.

I mean, of course I knew *how* it happened. I just couldn't believe that it had happened to *me*.

My heart had been ripped apart, both by rejection that seemed too much to bear and responsibility that seemed too much to carry.

All I wanted was to pinch myself and wake up from a life I couldn't believe was now mine.

Sometimes collisions happen because we drift, over time and unaware, until there is nothing left but the impact that shocks us awake.

At other times they happen because we stop paying attention to the beauty of our souls and the pulse of our existence. Damage can also happen when we make decisions that have consequences—some foreseeable, some not. Maybe you knew when you entertained a certain someone that it wasn't good for you, but you did it anyway. Maybe you took a job in another part of the country—an upward, positive move that now seems like the biggest mistake of your life. Or maybe you dedicated much of your time to caring for a loved one, and now that you're no longer that person's caregiver, you've lost your sense of direction.

Crash.

Impact.

Collision.

Choices result in outcomes of all shapes and sizes.

Let's face it. Some collisions are our own fault. We are encouraged to pay attention, drive carefully, and not take chances with our lives and the lives of those we love. Warnings all over the place beg us not to text and drive, statistics telling us that it can result in a crash or, worse, death, but people still do it.

Sometimes the responsibility for damage lies with multiple parties, making it difficult to assign blame or figure out where things started to go wrong. At what point did the marriage go sour? When did the breach between family members grow to the point that communication ceased? Why did the business partnership end in a catastrophe, leaving you figuring out how to pick up the pieces of your livelihood?

In other instances, the pain you feel and the brokenness you live with have nothing to do with you. You could be the victim of others' actions. When the person who chooses to drink and drive hits you or someone you love, it changes *your* life.

When the neighbor's son violated you, it affected *your* view of men, and your relationships with them too. When your mother critiqued you, when not even your very best was ever good enough, it caused *you* to feel as if you could never measure up. The cruel words other kids aimed at you found their mark. And when that man hit you with his own two hands the first time, you were stunned, but each time you chose to stay, you allowed your self-worth and value to be eroded bit by bit.

Maybe you suffer as a result of simply living this life. You lose your job. You can't move past the deep grief of a loved one. You find out you have cancer. Or the infertility treatments didn't work—again.

> Pay attention to the beauty of your soul and the pulse of your existence.

Or have you just quit living? No major catastrophe. You've just gotten tired of putting one foot in front of the other and *trying*. You are swept up by the whirlwind of just living your life, trying to keep up, desperately trying to make it. You are bored, exhausted, or done with trying to make something out of your life. It's just too much.

People often ask me what kept me going during that difficult season of my life. They wonder what helped me give birth to my baby, graduate from college, and hold myself together.

It was no walk in the park.

That season was indeed very hard.

But I also learned something during that time.

While there may be times when I feel that things cannot be repaired, they are never beyond repair when placed in the hands of the One who can make something out of nothing, mend what is broken, restore what seems unsalvageable.

It was in that place that God met me.

Right there.

The place where my drifts and decisions had led me.

The place where my lack of attention, intention, obedience, and common sense had dumped me.

The place where my soul, while still rare and beautiful, sat isolated, broken, and bruised. Where it seemed no one could reach me to help me, heal me, or guide me home.

He was there.

Even in that place where you feel most alone, most rejected, most powerless and without hope, that's where the love of God can be felt the deepest, experienced the most fully, and understood in the most beautifully unexpected way.

I was desperate. Desperate to believe that my life was salvageable. Desperate to know that I still could make good on my life. And more than finishing school, being in a relationship, getting a job, or finding happiness, I simply needed to find value in being me.

In that place of desperation, I picked up a Bible, searching for words from God's letter that would affirm my value in His eyes. One by one, I copied down verses that told me what He thought about me. I wrote those words on a piece of notebook paper and carried them around in my pocket, adding more Scriptures here and there as I discovered them.

One piece of paper became two, and then two became three. I stapled them together, folded them up, and carried those precious words with me at all times. Whenever I felt a pang of guilt, shame, or pain, I pulled out those verses and read them until I felt the love of God wash over me. If I found myself unable to control the tears that welled up throughout the day, I'd pull out the paper and read it again and again and again.

In that dark, desolate, damaged place, I learned the value of who I am because of *whose* I am.

As the daughter of a pastor who has heard sound doctrine and theology preached from the pulpit day in and day out, there is a lot that I know. I know that I am a created, crafted being. I know that I have value because that value was bestowed on me by someone greater. I know that I am loved.

But as a girl who struggled through difficult seasons, painful circumstances, and had been hurt by others; as someone who made bad choices, suffered the consequences, and gotten weary of living; as a person who studied the Bible, memorized parts of Scripture, and underlined and highlighted sections with different colored pens, this is what I also know:

It's not enough to know you are a unique, divinely created soul. You must *believe* it. And to believe it, you must choose to remember what you already know—or learn what you don't. Then you must choose to rehearse the idea of your value until it becomes so ingrained in your mind that it affects what you do, how you think, and the way you respond to what has occurred in your life, whether you caused it or not.

Whether you are a student of theology or haven't cracked open a Bible in years, this is the truth that forms the foundation for everything else in your life:

> **Your drifts, decisions, and collisions don't define you.**

You are loved.

Your drifts, decisions, and collisions don't define you. So if you feel lost in your life, grab hold of this truth and don't let it go.

You are loved.

Just the way you are.

Just where you are.

And God knows what to do to take you from where you are today to where He knows you can be tomorrow.

You are not just okay.

You are more than okay.

You are loved. You are accepted. You are valuable.

If you're struggling to believe that, pick up a Bible and search for words from God's letter to you that will affirm or reaffirm your value in His eyes. One by one, copy them down word-for-word, or paraphrase them in a way that is meaningful to you. Carry those words around with you and pull them out whenever you need to remember that you are loved.

> Learn to believe in the value of who you are because of whose you are. And never forget that you are loved.

Rehearse the idea of your value.

Believe the loving words from One who went to great lengths to make sure you are the only one of *you* there is.

I know that might be a daunting task, especially if you are in a really dark and lonely place, so let me get you started with a few that have been especially meaningful to me:

- "You are precious and honored in my sight, and . . . I love you" (Isa. 43:4).
- "I have loved you with an everlasting love" (Jer. 31:3).
- "You did not choose me, but I chose you" (John 15:16).

You, my friend, are loved.

Believe it.

Never forget it.

But if you find yourself feeling more broken and bruised because of the drifts, decisions, or collisions in your life, remember that even in those difficult dark places, He can be there with you. And the best part is He can make something of nothing, mend what is broken, and restore what seems unsalvageable.

So, my friend, despite your circumstances, learn to believe in the value of who you are because of whose you are.

And never forget that you are loved.

Reflections for the Rescue

REMEMBER

You are loved.

REFLECT

- As you were reading, what collision came to mind?
- What consequences are you facing from your past decisions? How have you been impacted by the decisions of others?
- No matter how bad things may be, nothing changes the fact that you are loved. Commit to rehearsing that idea until it sinks in.

RESPOND

Assemble your own list of verses that remind you of your value in God's eyes.

Genesis 21:17–19; Genesis 50:20;
Isaiah 41:10; Jeremiah 31:3; Zephaniah 3:14–17;
John 3:16; 2 Corinthians 1:9–11; Revelation 3:9.

PRECIOUS CARGO

Carry Your Contents Carefully

F ast-forward twenty years from my college days.
Marriage. Five kids. Family road trip.

My husband had been driving for most of our four-hour trip back home, but he was clearly exhausted. As much as I loved reading and relaxing in the passenger seat next to him, I offered to take over the driving so he could have a break. There was only another hour left of our journey, and while I felt a little tired, I figured I could make it to our neck of the woods without incident.

About fifteen minutes from home, I was fighting to keep my eyes open. The sandman had sneaked up on me. My body felt heavy and my eyes were burning. I felt as if I'd gulped down half a bottle of Benadryl. All of the tried-and-true tactics for staying awake had been attempted. The radio was blaring. I was sitting straight up, forcibly and rhythmically tapping the wheel with my hands. I moved my legs violently back and forth, willing my adrenaline to keep me awake.

On the last major stretch home, I stopped at a red light. Grateful for a moment of respite, I closed my eyes for just a minute.

Let's just say they were closed for more than a minute.

I woke up to loud banging on the driver's side window. With a glance,

I noticed that the light was still red, but a police officer was standing outside my window. Clueless as to what he might want, I rolled down the window.

"Ma'am? Are you okay?"

"Yes, officer. I'm fine."

"Do you know where you are?"

"Uh, yes, officer." I stated the city, state, and road at his request. (What is it with public servants always wanting me to verify I'm in my right mind?)

"Ma'am? Do you know how long you've been stopped at this light?"

"Not exactly, officer, but I just stopped at the red light and closed my eyes for a second." A slow panic rose in the pit of my stomach and made its way up to my chest.

"Well, ma'am, I don't know how long you've been here either, but it's been long enough for the police department to receive multiple calls about a lady who was either passed out or dead at this here stoplight—and long enough for me to make my way here from my last call."

Whaaaaaat?!

Apparently my attempt to rest my eyes had resulted in my falling asleep at the wheel. I had not passed out. I wasn't dead. But neither was I awake or alert, both of which are necessary for being behind the wheel.

"Who else is in the car, ma'am?"

"Just my family. We're on our way back from a road trip. I'm only a few minutes from home."

"And you haven't been drinking?"

"No, sir."

"Or taking drugs?"

"No, sir."

So glad he believed me and didn't make me get out of the car to prove any of that to him. I guess driving a minivan has its perks.

"Well, ma'am, do you think you can make it to your house?"

Of course I could make it home fully alert and awake with no problem whatsoever—a policeman was standing at my car door! Now adrenaline pulsed through my body—no violent leg shaking required.

"Yes, sir. I'm awake. I can make it home."

"Ma'am, you've *got* to make it home. You need to wake up. Drive responsibly. You are carrying precious cargo. It's your duty to be mindful of what's inside and get the contents of your vehicle safely to its destination."

I turned to look at the people I loved, who were, for the most part, still sleeping soundly. That gave me a moment of clarity. Possibility rested within my control, and it was my duty to stay awake to care well for the future of all who lay inside.

I thanked the officer for the wake-up call and, with renewed focus and resolve, finished the drive home. But I've never forgotten those words.

"Ma'am, you've *got* to make it home."

The police officer's words have reverberated in my mind and heart many times since that night. And they often bear repeating.

You need to wake up.

Drive responsibly.

You, my friend, are carrying precious cargo.

> You, my friend, are carrying precious cargo.

You, my friend, have a job to do.

It is your responsibility to move through your life well so that you can make it to the destination that represents home for you.

While this concept can extend to things you touch—your family, friends, or responsibilities—right now, I'm talking about you.

What's inside of you. And everything that makes you *you*.

While you may be tired, distracted, or just taking a break from living with focus or resolve, you're not dead. It is my desire to call you to attention and beg you to live alert, be responsible, and operate in full awareness of the possibilities that lie within you.

Does God love you? Yes, He does.

Do you have value? Yes, you do.

But if you won't operate on those truths, you're not unleashing their power in your life.

⁓

We're going to dive in to acting on truth in just a sec, but first let's talk about a crucial point.

You can't simply read the words of encouragement that I write in this book—or the words inspired by God Himself in the Bible—and merely know them. You must believe them to the point of taking action. Knowledge that does not result in action is simply information.

Just because you know doesn't mean you grow.

It is your willingness to engage with what you've seen, heard, or understood that changes you and influences the way your life unfolds.

The way you think about yourself is the starting point of renewing your actions. Proverbs 23:7 says, "For as he thinks within himself, so he is" (NASB). How you think affects what you do.

> Just because you know doesn't mean you grow.

It's one thing to hear and comprehend that you are loved by God. It's another thing to appreciate and be grateful for that love. But it's a whole 'nother thing to believe that truth enough to receive it, accept it, and then act on it.

Action based on belief changes you from the inside out.

Hear. Understand. Believe.

Then act like what you believe is true.

Awaken to the value that you have been provided and stay alert.

It is *your* duty to discover, know well, and remain aware of what's inside you. It is *your* assignment to steward what you've been given. It is *your* job to get the contents within you deposited safely at their destination. It is *your* duty to love yourself enough to live with hope, intention, and focus.

And just in case you are tempted to feel guilty about the idea of self-love and self-care, let me let you off the hook a bit. In the words of Joyce Meyer, "We should love ourselves—not in a selfish, self-centered way that produces a lifestyle of self-indulgence, but in a balanced, godly way, a way that simply affirms God's creation as essentially good and right."[8]

God did His part by loving you first (1 John 4:19), but you do your part when you choose to receive that love by being rooted and grounded in it (Eph. 3:17) and loving yourself enough to take your precious life seriously.

Now, I know somebody might be disagreeing with me here and saying, "Nope! I'm not behind the wheel. *Jesus* is behind the wheel. I'm supposed to let Him take control while I sit in the passenger seat and let Him direct everything in my life!"

Try for just a second to get Carrie's song out of your head. (By the way, I love Carrie's song. And yes, I'm talking about Carrie Underwood like I know her on a first-name basis.)

Yes, God wants to guide and direct you, but He doesn't live through you *apart* from you. He's given you what you need, but you have a role to play and a job to do. You are a recipient of God's grace (Phil. 1:7), but He wants you to respond to His call on your life (Heb. 3:1). You have everything you need to do this because you also share His divine nature (2 Peter 1:4).

You have to participate consistently and intentionally in your life. That's your job.

Never forget that *you* are behind the wheel. Your choice to live with acute awareness is the key to getting where you've been designed to go.

If you don't choose to be alert and attentive, it's easy to drift, make decisions that halt your progress, or even cause a collision. And if you don't value your individuality, you will find it difficult to see worth in the fragments or debris left after someone has collided with you.

I want to make this as clear as I can.

It is your job in this life to know and value what makes you *you* and to treasure the opportunity you have to make a distinct impression with this one life you have.

No one else can do this for you.

Sure, other people might encourage you, call things out of you, or help you along the way by lighting your path, but the responsibility of carrying your contents carefully is yours.

> It's your job to participate consistently and intentionally in your life.

Never forget, my friend, that your God-given life is yours to live.

First hear. Know and receive God's perspective about how precious you are to Him. Then understand. Pay attention to your cargo. Gain a fresh perspective on the value that God has placed in you. Finally, believe. Allow what you hear and understand to saturate how you see yourself and the world in which you live.

Then choose to act as if what you say you believe is true.

Reflections for the Rescue

REMEMBER

You, my friend, are carrying precious cargo.

REFLECT

- Have you been living alertly, responsibly, and fully aware? If so, how do you know? If not, why do you think that is?
- Do you think you have been a good steward of your life thus far? Why or why not?
- Do you struggle with loving yourself based on the love that God has for you? Why or why not?

RESPOND

- Identify your biggest struggle in carrying your cargo well: (1) hearing: "I don't know God's perspective about me," (2) understanding: "I don't know or love my God-given cargo well," (3) believing: "I don't always act as if what I know and understand is true."
- Pinpoint one thing you can do this week to participate intentionally in your life, particularly in the area where you seem to struggle most.

Isaiah 43:4; Isaiah 49:5; Matthew 10:29–31;
Luke 12:7; Psalm 8:4–5; 1 Peter 2:9.

GAIN PERSPECTIVE

Look and Listen

Not long after the day I begged God to break both of my legs, I left my job. I don't think I made it even a year. I figured it was better to spend a few weeks looking for a new job than looking out of a hospital window.

While I wasn't sure what to do next, I knew that I wanted to pause to take a fresh look at my life. So, one afternoon, I made a cup of hot tea, then sat with pen in hand and thought about what in me might still be valuable, useful, and notable.

On a blank sheet of paper, I wrote the words "strengths," "weaknesses," "passions," and "personality traits." I underlined each word and sat pensively, staring at the page while waiting for my thoughts to flow.

I was a little disillusioned with how my life had gone so far, but I decided to take inventory so I could figure out where to go next. I thought that I'd headed in the wrong direction in my career because I hadn't carefully identified the cargo I was carrying and aligned that knowledge with an appropriate destination.

Honestly, it wasn't just about the job.

I wanted to put down on paper the parts of me I'd forgotten about, walked away from, dismissed, or devalued because of drifts, decisions, and collisions.

I struggled at first to write much down. I didn't realize how much my self-destructive thoughts, habits, and actions had affected me. I had a hard time finding "the gift of me" underneath the rubble of my circumstances and the debris of painful experiences.

But I sat. I looked. I listened.

After awhile, a few words came. They didn't come fast, but they came.

I kept listening. And I persisted in writing down the thoughts that came to mind. While I didn't get much on paper that first day, I kept the piece of paper near and pulled it out here and there. I slowly realized how important it was to pay attention to the unique material God had given me to work with and to think about my life. The more I took the time to notice, the more I noticed was there.

Over time, the list grew, one word at a time, until I'd uncovered more of what God had given me than what I'd buried.

Twenty years ago (Lord have mercy, has it been that long?), I asked myself a series of questions to gain a new perspective on my life. I didn't know then what I know now, but I realized that in order to change my life, I was going to have to do something different. These questions allowed me to take inventory of my situation and the state of my soul. In trying to figure out what I was good at, capable of, interested in, and excited about, I was taking stock of the gift of me and the gifts God had given me to use in this world. And in doing so, I also took responsibility for living my life well.

> In order to change your life, you are going to have to do something different.

That's your responsibility too.

Now, what I intended to do here was list a bunch of questions—many of the same questions I asked myself twenty years ago—and ask you to break out a pen and do the work right here in this chapter.

But I own a book like that. It's a good book. When reading it, though,

I skipped all the pages with the questions because I didn't want to stop the conversation I was having with the author.

So in the interest of keeping you reading, I've sprinkled just a few questions here to get your juices flowing but added more questions for personal assessment at the end of this book. Turn there now if you feel like thinking or turn there later when you're ready to do some soul work.

GAIN a New Perspective

Have you ever taken the time to think about—and maybe even document—the God-given contents you're carrying? God expects us to discover, develop, and deploy our gifts as we live this life. While God gives us life, we honor Him by using what He's placed inside. We show appreciation when we develop our abilities and skills. We live fully when we make room for our interests and passions. And we gain clarity when we take stock of our nature—our personality, character, and temperament.

> God expects us to discover, develop, and deploy our gifts as we live this life.

The problem is we get busy living and forget to look at the life He's given us.

Soon after I quit my first job out of college, I made the time to look, mostly out of disappointment and frustration. The exercise was not very refined, but it was real. I'd decided to pay attention, listen to my life, and gain a fresh perspective on what God had put in me.

Gifts

I started out listing my gifts. I brainstormed my strengths—areas I was naturally good at. I thought about activities that came easily to me. I knew I was a good listener and a strategic planner. I loved solving problems and figuring things out. Organizing information or people always seemed to be a piece of cake, and words . . . well, I loved words and had a knack for using them.

What about you? What comes easily or naturally to you that does not come easily for others?

Abilities

After listing my areas of natural giftedness, I took stock of my areas of natural ability—things that I didn't necessarily think I had a gift for doing, but that I was capable of doing. Abilities are things you learn to do. They are skills that may or may not come naturally but that you develop over time. I felt like my skills and abilities had led me right to the job I didn't like, so I enlisted help. Sometimes other people can see our abilities better than we can, so I asked friends and family to tell me what abilities they saw in me that might help me earn a living.

Between my thoughts and their input, I wrote down a list of my abilities, which included stuff like being good with numbers, having strong organizational skills, and having an aptitude for playing the piano.

What are you capable of doing? What skills have you learned or developed over time?

Interests

Having a gift or an ability to do something doesn't necessarily mean you enjoy it.

I'd ended up in my first job out of college because I was a problem solver who was good with numbers. Yet being good at or capable of doing something wasn't enough to keep me from losing my mind.

I realized that I desperately desired to be interested in what I did every day. While I wasn't sure if my job would be the place where I could truly engage my interests, I realized that I hadn't really cultivated them at work or in my personal life.

So I asked myself what I enjoyed doing and what interests I wanted to develop, practice, or enjoy without coercion. If given spare time, how would I spend it? Thinking about this, I realized that numbers weren't enough. I needed to have contact with people and be in a position to help them.

What do you like to do? What do you gravitate toward when you have the space and time to do what makes your soul smile?

Nature

Apart from what I was gifted, able, or interested in doing, I put some thought into my nature—the qualities that form my character and personality. Who I am and what I'm like consistently influence my reputation. What would I say about me if I were recommending myself to another person?

Honestly, I needed help with this one. I'd taken a personality test in high school, so I pulled that out to give me the language with which to talk to myself about myself. Since then I've taken two or three other tests. I know that learning about me is a lifelong journey and that sometimes getting information from other sources—people or tests—is helpful.

What qualities do you consistently represent? What words would you use to describe your personality?

It Takes Time

My effort to GAIN a new perspective wasn't done in a day. I added to that Word document over a period of weeks as I collected my thoughts and gathered input from others.

But once I was done, I was able to more clearly articulate both to myself and others the gifts that God had given me.

I had more clarity about the precious cargo inside.

It takes time.

Twenty years later, I've made time here and there for this exercise whenever I feel lost or out of touch with how God has made me. I don't always have all the answers or know how to fill in all the blanks. The beauty is I don't have to have it all figured out to move forward.

But here's what I do know. The more conscious I am about whose I am, the better I get at fully expressing who I am.

Whether or not you choose to go through this exercise, I hope you listen to your life and do the work of recognizing the value of what's inside. My prayer is that you let that knowledge keep you awake and alert at the wheel.

I'll always remember the officer who woke me up at the stoplight. He asked me something important.

> You don't have to have it all figured out to move forward.

He asked me who was in the car and, in doing so, helped me to focus. When I turned and looked over my shoulder to see my family, I was reminded that my duty to drive with care was based on something deeply important.

When you are attentive to the life you carry inside—the potential power of all the possible words *you* can speak, actions *you* can take, and moments *you* can create—that awareness greatly affects how determined you are to focus on your journey.

Remember, God has placed value on your life, but it's your job to be aware of that value and be willing to act on it.

If you truly believe you are uniquely designed, then the question begs asking: Have you taken the time to *look* at your design and listen to the heartbeat of who you are? And have you done it recently? The first step in your journey of self-discovery is to pay attention to what makes you *you*—right here and right now.

When I look inside the contents of my soul, I gain clarity about my cargo. I'm reminded that possibility rests within my control and that it's my duty to care well for what has been entrusted to me.

While initially driven to GAIN a new perspective on my job situation, I now know that making time to ponder helped me to be a better steward of my time in many areas of my life.

And time is the most precious commodity I have.

Knowing that living aware means maintaining consistent focus, I resolve to remember who I am and to learn more about God's gifts to me along the journey.

And it is in living with focus and resolve based on the precious cargo in me that I will be able to make it home to the plans and purposes God has for my life.

Let me encourage you to make the time to look and to listen. Grab some hot tea or coffee, a cold diet soda, or whatever you enjoy. Grab a pen and a sheet of paper. Give yourself the space to think. And please know that you don't have to have all the answers or fill in all the blanks right away. You don't have to have it all figured out to move forward. You just need to live aware, resolving to learn more about God's gifts to you along the way.

You are a soul. And no matter where you've been or how far you've traveled, there is still precious cargo in you. As you live your life, your job, my friend, is to do the work of discovering, developing, and deploying "the gift of you."

Reflections for the Rescue

REMEMBER

Discover, develop, and deploy the gifts in you.

REFLECT

- What parts of yourself have you forgotten, walked away from, dismissed, or devalued?
- Are you acting on the gifts, abilities, interests, and nature you are aware of? Why or why not?
- Why do you think we tend to avoid making time to look at our lives? Why is it important to do so?

RESPOND

- Take some time to think about—and even document—the God-given gifts inside of you.
- Ask friends or family members to tell you what they see in you. Often other people who know us can see things in us we don't see in ourselves.

2 Peter 1:4; Ephesians 3:17; Philippians 1:7;
2 Corinthians 9:15; 1 John 4:19.

WAKE UP AND DRIVE

Participate in the Process

I'm used to driving past E.

My husband loves cars, and there was a season when he bought used cars at an auction with the intent to sell them. That meant I was driving a different car every few months.

That also meant I had to test the car to see how far past E it would go—specifically, once the yellow light came on, exactly how many miles I could still drive before running out of gas.

No sense in letting the light freak you out if you really have twenty miles left in the tank.

Sure, I paid attention to the car so I noticed when it started acting funny or making weird sounds—sounds that indicated it might be on the last drop of fuel. My time-tested method of learning what the yellow E light *really* meant worked most of the time.

But once, when my husband was out of town, I got in the latest auction car, a big red Suburban, put the keys in the ignition, and got nothing.

In a little bit of a panic, I came up with a not-so-ingenious solution. I grabbed my oldest daughter, who was twelve years old, and told her to get behind the wheel and closely follow my instructions. Slowly and carefully, I pushed that red Suburban down our neighborhood street to the corner gas station and instructed my twelve-year-old to turn in to the entrance.

Under normal circumstances, I never would have put my twelve-year-old behind the wheel.

Under normal circumstances, I never would have pushed a doggone Suburban down my street.

But guess what?

I was out of gas.

And I wasn't going anywhere.

If you don't take care of the car you're driving, don't be surprised if the cargo in it isn't moving forward.

Driving responsibly means you have to pay attention to the vehicle.

You accomplish what you accomplish here on this earth through the vehicle of your body. Your hands, feet, mouth, ears, eyes, and nose all assist you in an infinite number of ways as you accomplish tasks, serve others, and make your mark on the world.

Taking care of your body requires effort and discipline. Elisabeth Elliot says, "Discipline, for the Christian, begins with the body. We have only one. It is this body that is the primary material given to us for sacrifice. We cannot give our hearts to God and keep our bodies for ourselves."

It is true that your body is temporary. It is not designed to last forever. Each and every day, your body moves one step closer to its inevitable end. So it stands to reason that if you care about your soul, you should care about the body that carries your soul around.

Plain English?

You have to take care of yourself.

Because the body is temporary, it can be tempting not to put in the effort to care for it. The thinking goes like this: "What's on the inside is really what matters, so I don't want to place an inappropriate emphasis on something that only has an interim role." But if your body plays a major part in how you impact your world, it does indeed need some TLC.

Let's discuss the elephant in the room. If you struggle with your weight, I know this statement might make you nervous. Trust me. I'm the queen of all things "Thirty Day," "Slim Trim," "Quick Fast," and "I hope this will last." I know the battle of the bulge is real, and it's not easy to conquer.

But you only get this one body. If you want it to last, you have to treat it right. Eating well and maintaining a healthy level of physical activity in your life are forms of self-respect. Your choice to take care of your temple shows that you have an appreciation of how very precious you are.

No guilt or judgment here. Just encouragement to keep in mind that you matter.

All of you.

Beyond the fight with the #fatdemon, your body is affected by stress, worry, lack of sleep, bitterness, unforgiveness, and unresolved emotional trauma.

Taking care of your body involves a holistic view of what impacts your physical ability to keep up, to make good on what fills you, completes you, and gives you energy for your journey.

I'm not pushing *Sports Illustrated* model here, because Lord knows my behind *ain't eva* gonna fit nice and neat into those bikinis some women wear. I'm saying that you and I both need to do whatever it takes to give our frames of flesh the opportunity to best express who we are inside. We simply cannot give our best when we press our bodies to the limit. And even if we think we can give 110 percent today, we won't be able to keep it up for very long.

Don't be so engrossed in the business of living your life that you forget to take care of your body.

If you are sick and have health challenges beyond your control, I know how frustrating it can be to have physical limitations—especially when your mind and heart yearn to do more than what your body will allow. The migraines, arthritis, fibromyalgia, blood pressure, back trouble, or multiple sclerosis can seem to undermine your deepest desires, hopes, and dreams.

But even with chronic illness, you still can choose to give yourself the best opportunity to live at *your* physical capacity and release the full strength of what's inside.

The car I'm driving now is getting older. It's a minivan. I drive it because I always have a bunch of kids in the car, which means it's not in pristine condition. There are some stains that won't ever come all the way out, a tear in back of the right passenger seat, and my husband just told me that the shocks are leaking—whatever that means.

> Don't be so engrossed in the business of living your life that you forget to take care of your body.

I try my best to keep up with the maintenance, but some things I just won't fix—like the tear in the back seat or the paint that's losing its luster. We live in that car. We use it every stinkin' day. Even if I wanted to keep the car forever, even if I intended to repair everything that could ever go wrong with it, it will eventually fall apart. It's a car. It's not designed to last forever. That's why it's called a depreciating asset.

I know we girls don't like to think about it, but this is the truth.

Your body is a depreciating asset.

It's not designed to last forever. But while the real you, the soul of you, lives in your body and your life blood pulses within, it is your duty to do your best to take care of it, keep it presentable, and put in the effort to make it last. "Don't you realize that your body is the temple of the Holy Spirit, who lives in you and was given to you by God? You do not belong to yourself, for God bought you with a high price. So you must honor God with your body" (1 Cor. 6:19–20 NLT).

We women have a habit of taking care of everyone else but ourselves.

Some of us need permission to take care of us. Well, I'm giving you permission to take care of you. Listen to your body. Know when you're low on fuel. Maintain your health.

Go to the doctor. Drop the weight. Get enough sleep. Get enough sun. Get more exercise. Drink more water. Eat clean. Resist worry. Reduce stress. Slow down. And breathe deeply.

And while you're taking care of the inside, don't forget to keep the outside clean, presentable, neat, and maybe a tad shined up. There is nothing wrong with allowing the beauty of what's inside you to overflow to the outside.

But never forget, no matter how precious the cargo is or how shined up the exterior may be, it won't move if there is no power.

Your soul is designed to be filled with abundant life—life that comes from the living Spirit.

You are a soul that functions in a spiritual way, designed to be fully alive only when you are filled to overflowing with life that bubbles up with the Spirit of God. There is no one like you, and you have the power of the God of all yesterdays and today and forever who is willing to help you.

> Your soul is designed to be filled with abundant life—life that comes from the living Spirit.

But without the living Spirit of God operating in and through your one-of-a-kind life, you can function, but your life will not have power. Sure, you can do good things and operate in spiritual ways and have a decent life without God—lots of people do. You can purpose to have positive thinking, better your behaviors, and search out the seemingly spiritual. However, without the power of God operating in your life, you cannot have a useful and fruitful life and participate in His plans that will matter most for eternity.

If you believe in God and in His son, Jesus Christ, then the Spirit of God lives in you. A part of the benefit, so to speak, of trusting in the death and resurrection of Christ is that you don't just get to have a relationship with the God of the universe; the God of the universe *lives* in you! You get the chance to have a fulfilling soul-rich experience on earth, and the living Spirit of God in you will allow your soul to have the exact same thing in heaven.

Just like the power of the engine in your car, the power of the Spirit of God is available to you. But here's the rub: it's up to you whether you are *filled* with the Holy Spirit.

To be filled with the Spirit, you must regularly invite God into your life by flooding your mind and thoughts with God's perspective—a perspective He makes clear in His Word. You invite God in when you pray, talking and listening to Him throughout your day. You invite God's power when you allow Him to show you what He wants you to do with the precious cargo He gave you.

I'm convinced that living with an eye on the important requires a consistent awareness of what God is doing and being willing to join Him on the path He has planned for you.

Let me offer you a simple solution to the problem of living with consistency and intentionality. Since the problem that I'm describing in this chapter is not a lack of knowledge but a lack of consistent engagement with the truth, the solution lies in figuring out how to connect regularly with what you know.

Luke 9:23 says, "If anyone wishes to come after Me, he must deny himself, and take up his cross *daily* and follow Me" (NASB, emphasis mine).

The key to staying awake is to daily decide to focus on what is important—what God wants you to do, where God wants you to go, and who God wants you to be.

Some years ago, a mentor advised me to get up every morning, stretch my hands to heaven before my feet hit the floor, and offer God my mind, my heart, and my day. I still do this often.

But I have to tell you that I struggle with consistency. As much as I want to stay awake and alert to the value of my life, my tendency is to get lulled to sleep, to take breaks, and to forget. So recently, I've decided to be tactical about remembering to do this.

I've put a reminder on my phone to check in with God on a daily basis. My phone chimes every morning with a message that reads, "Ask God what He wants me to do today." I have this prayer typed in the reminder as a note: "Lord, today I surrender my will to Your way. Help me to be an instrument of Your grace, love, mercy, and power."

I figure that if He has a plan every day for what He is doing in the world, I should ask Him every day to show me what role He wants me to play, how He would have me participate, and what He might want me to do with the precious cargo that He's given me to carry.

In *Heavenly Help: Experiencing the Holy Spirit in Everyday Life*, Sarah Bowling says, "When all the dust settles, there is no one with whom you are more authentically yourself than the Spirit of truth. No one knows you better than the Holy Spirit . . . With the Holy Spirit, you live in complete truth."[9]

You can take a lifetime getting to know yourself through the lessons your journey brings, or you can take a shortcut by believing that the One who uniquely created you also has a thing or two to say about who you are and what you should do "with your one wild and precious life."[10]

I can't tell you how freeing it is to know that I have help. I don't have to generate my own power. I don't have to figure everything out on my own. This life that I have and the journey to becoming the person I want to be are major undertakings. How beautiful to know that both because of my unique design and through the Designer alive in me, I have everything that I need to live well. "For His divine power has bestowed on us [absolutely] everything necessary for [a dynamic spiritual] life and godliness, through true and personal knowledge of Him who called us by His own glory and excellence" (2 Peter 1:3 AMP).

All people are spiritual by design. We are awed beyond what we see because of what we sense. We crave deep meaningful connection and, because of this, we often search for it in the created rather than in the Creator. But if you can grasp and understand that your soul has a secret weapon in the person of the Holy Spirit, who wants to express His power through you, that knowledge simply changes the game and opens up a world of possibility. You can know more than you actually know because the one who knows all lives in you. You just have to stay awake and alert to His work in you.

Staying awake to your life requires your participation. While God provides the engine, the tools, and the time, you have to dig in and do the work. No one else can do it for you. God is all powerful, all knowing, and all sufficient, but God also uses people.

He wants to use you, but you have to be willing to do your part.

To use my daddy's illustration (yes, I'm totally stealing it with no shame), God did His job when He put under the hood everything you need to live your life. You have life. You breathe, you move, and you have this gorgeous, distinct, remarkably individual soul. But, girl . . . *you* have to get behind the wheel, push the pedal, and drive. You have to do the work of seeking directions, following instructions, staying awake, and keeping your eyes on the road.

> God is all powerful, all knowing, and all sufficient, but God also uses people.

Your life depends on it.

Doing the work of being awake isn't always going to be easy, but it is important. *You* are important. Taking care of you—soul, body, and spirit—is a necessity.

I'm not telling you this because I've always done it perfectly. I've done it all wrong a lot of my life. You would think that after the difficult season of teenage pregnancy, experiencing God's love and acceptance, and getting back on my feet, I would have figured out that it was worth my effort to steer clear of drifts, decisions, and collisions. You would think that I would have done everything in my power to live wide awake and look intently for distractions that derail and prohibit movement in the right direction.

I didn't.

I'm sad to say that I've spent too much time going in circles. On again, off again. Up, down, and around. It takes effort, discipline, and determination to stay awake at the wheel. Many times, I opted to take a break, rest on my laurels, or speed down some random road—in reverse. The times I've gotten lost, I can now look back and see that I quit participating, in some way, with what God had deposited in me, directions He had given me, or hope He had offered me.

Have you ever felt like you've wasted time, taken chances, or put the best of who you are on the altar of convenience, the desire to live carefree, or some craving that is only temporarily filled? Or maybe because the road has been hard, the collisions have hurt too badly, or the distance to cover has seemed too great, you've simply given up.

Well, it's my hope that I can save you some time and encourage you to stay awake and live aware.

Living your life well is your responsibility—your responsibility to God and to yourself. God is not going to make you play a starring role in your own life. You have to show up and do your part.

You have to participate in the process of your self-discovery.

Every now and then He may allow someone, something, or some circumstance in your life to jolt you awake and remind you that you need to fight to stay present in your journey. But it is your job to realize that what you are carting around every day is a gift. If you needed a loud rap on the window and a jolt of adrenaline to get you going, this is it.

Now let's wake up and drive.

Reflections for the Rescue

REMEMBER

Staying awake to your life requires your participation.

REFLECT

- On a scale of 1 to 10, how would you rate the care that you give your body?
- In what specific ways can you do a better job of caring for your self?
- Is the Spirit of God operating in your life? How do you know?
- What do you do to invite God into your life? How do you connect with His perspective and power?

RESPOND

Identify two habits you would like to be more consistent in—one spiritual and one physical. Ask someone who loves you to hold you accountable to doing so.

BODY: *1 Corinthians 6:19; 1 Corinthians 15:42; Philippians 2:12–13; Matthew 5:16; Ephesians 2:10; Romans 12:1–2.*

SPIRIT: *Galatians 5:16; Ephesians 5:18; John 16:13–15; John 14:16–17; Colossians 3:23; 1 Corinthians 3:16; John 14:26; Romans 15:13; 1 Thessalonians 5:6.*

FOLLOW THE YELLOW CRUMB ROAD

You Don't Have to Know It All

We have a rule in my house about eating in the kitchen. All of the food stays in the kitchen because I don't want to go all over the house cleaning up after people. I try really hard not to clean up after people. I call my kids out of their rooms—or out of their beds at night, if necessary—to clean up what they messed up.

Call me a mean mom.

It's okay. I'm used to it.

But on that rare occasion when one of my kiddos gets bold enough to sneak something out of the kitchen and into the living area, it doesn't remain a secret for long.

Why?

Because they leave a trail, like an empty wrapper, a sticky spot on the floor, or crumbs.

When my kids were smaller, they were infamous for leaving a trail of crumbs. They didn't mean to; it was just in their nature to do so. Those crumbs were inevitable, especially when they would get hold of some of those dadgum Cheez-Its.

Wait, have you ever had the White Cheddar Cheez-Its? They are like crack. I could eat a whole box by myself!

My babies would stick their whole hand inside the box and walk off with little squares sticking out between their fingers. They couldn't hold all the cheesy goodness without letting a few crumbs, or maybe even a whole cracker or two, spill out of their grasp.

If the little cracker criminal was bold enough to walk freely around my house, I'd always know exactly where to find him by following his trail.

I just had to pay attention to the crumbs.

Did you know that God has been gracious enough to leave us crumbs? It's true, and it's a good thing. These crumbs are signs of His guidance that He places before us to take notice of.

It's in His nature to do so. Psalm 37:23 says, "The LORD directs the steps of the godly. He delights in every detail of their lives" (NLT).

God enjoys seeing us live out the details of our lives, and He helps us on the way by leaving us a trail of crumbs right in plain sight to follow.

Even when we feel lost in life, there's always a way out! The first and most obvious of those crumbs are the words that He has taken care, over thousands of years, to make available for our instruction. Psalm 119:133 says, "Direct my footsteps according to your word; let no sin rule over me."

Let me be clear here.

Many of the places where I have felt the most lost came as a result of my choice not to follow the trail He had already made clear. I am so thankful that working my way back from the drifts, decisions, or collisions because of those choices wasn't a guessing game. It simply started with knowing and acting on the words God shared in His letter of love.

There have been times when I've felt lost for no reason of my own doing. At times, another person's choices have affected me. Other times, I simply felt that way because that's what happens in life—every now and again we have no idea where we should go next. The good news is that the same God who knows all and takes pleasure in the details of my life has provided words of healing and hope to meet me in those places too.

Most exciting, beyond the hope and healing, He provides hints for setting me back on course.

In my early twenties, I took the time to look inside at what God had given me by starting to follow the trail He left for me. He put words together in a book to share His thoughts for a well-lived life for *every* person. Then He left hints for me to do the living only I can do.

We can't see our path, my friend, if we don't look in *two* places—what God has said in His Word for revelation to all and also what He has placed in us individually that directs our lives according to our gifts, abilities, interests, and natures.

Now, I don't mean to sound all superspiritual here. Trust me. There have been many seasons of my life when I wish I'd been more spiritually minded and more consistent in acting on the principles I'm sharing with you here. But that's what I love about God. He has kept on loving and leading me even when I haven't always been as faithful as I could have been.

And He is always loving and leading you too.

Just follow the crumbs.

Noticing God's guidance doesn't have to be difficult. In my life, I've seen His direction at work in very simple ways.

In my twenties, after gaining a new perspective on what God had given me, what *did* I know about myself? What breadcrumbs were easy for me to see?

Well, I liked numbers. But I didn't like working in my job because I like working with numbers *while* working with people. So I looked for an opportunity to change jobs. That meant making substantially less money, but I also experienced less stress and more peace.

I also knew that I loved achievement. I liked working toward a goal. At my new job there were a series of licenses that were beneficial for me to obtain. I took every single test that I could, and I experienced a great sense of accomplishment.

In addition, I loved helping people. So I got really good at talking with clients and working hard to meet their expectations. I found satisfaction in knowing that I was of service to another person and that they were a little better off after interacting with me.

So what kind of job did I find that gave me a sense of peace, accomplishment, and satisfaction? A customer service job—a job that kept me tethered to the phone lines of a mutual fund company.

Whadya know.

The job that was the lowest-paying job I've ever had in my adult life is also a job that I greatly enjoyed. I kept working to develop my abilities based on the crumbs God allowed me to discover, and I followed those crumbs step by step where they led.

That job also provided the foundation for another employment opportunity that I also loved. (That next job happened to pay significantly more money too!) But I never would have had that opportunity if I hadn't looked at how God made me and acted on the intel.

Today, I don't work in the numbers business at all, but everything I learned about business and dealing with people still serves me well. Did I know I would be the financial manager of my home and that my husband would trust me to oversee our finances and make decisions about how we invest our money? Nope! Did I know I'd one day be running my own business? Nope, I had no idea. But I can tell you that I lived and I learned. The crumbs are never just about the crumbs; they're about following a trail that leads somewhere. Everything I learned then serves me well now.

Don't despise the crumbs. It's never *just* about the crumbs. It's always about where the crumbs might lead. So don't despise the small steps you can take or belittle small things.

You never know how God can use where you are right now to lead you to where He wants you to be.

The good news is you don't have to know where the trail leads in order to follow it. You just have to go with what you know.

> Don't despise the small steps you can take.

One of the things I love about the story of Moses in the Bible is that, in hindsight, it's very clear how God led Moses to the place of leading God's people, the Israelites.

In Exodus 2, we read about Moses and his passion for the Hebrew people. Even though he was raised as Egyptian royalty, Moses was so passionate that he murdered an Egyptian who whipped a Hebrew slave.

After running for fear of his life into the desert, Moses no longer lived a life of royalty but instead took on the lowly position of a shepherd. He led sheep. Moses learned in exile how to take care of animals that aren't known for being the sharpest tacks. He got practice caring for those who needed constant guidance and direction.

So when God shows up in the burning bush in Exodus 3 and tells Moses it's time to lead the Hebrew people into freedom, Moses is confused. How could God be asking him to do such a thing when he was such a sinful, simple, unsophisticated soul?

God saw what Moses didn't.

He saw Moses' passion and personality as well as the profession he had developed as things that He could use.

Can't you see it?

I'm guessing that it's easier for you to see it with Moses' story than it is to see it with your own. That's the problem, isn't it? It's always so easy to see the trail of breadcrumbs in someone else's life.

It's also easy to see our own crumbs in hindsight.

But right now, in this moment, you might feel like you have absolutely no idea where you are or where you're headed.

That's okay! *You* are okay, remember?

God will never leave you without a next step. He leaves you hints for what to do next.

Evidence.

Breadcrumbs.

This is such good news if you've never had a clear vision of who you wanted the girl inside you to be. You serve a God who knows you better than you know yourself and wants you to fol-low the breadcrumbs so He can surprise you with who He *knows* you can be!

Let me give you an example.

In the second grade, I found myself in the middle of an effort to bring world peace to the

> **God will never leave you without a next step.**

school playground and do my part to break up a catfight between two girls from my class. Nobody asked for my help, but there's something in my DNA that doesn't like to see unnecessary anguish, anger, or heart-ache. I recall feeling as if it were my duty to help them make peace because if they had peace, then our class would have peace, and we'd have a better classroom if we could all be on the same page. Simple enough, right? In my second-grade brain, it totally made sense that I would spend part of recess with one girl on one end of the playground hearing her side of the story, then walk to the other end to do the same with the other girl.

Fast-forward to high school, where in the church youth group I always seemed to have ideas for how we could make things better and experience more community. I felt like it was my duty to meet with the leaders of the youth group, present my thoughts, and then help implement everything I'd presented. My goal was to create a collective experience that would benefit everybody.

Later, as a mom at home with young children, I lamented the fact that none of my friends lived on my street. Every house nearby was empty because the other moms were at work, and I felt very alone. And so I jumped online and invited a bunch of my other stay-at-home-mommy friends to join me in an email group so we could chat throughout the day like neighbors would. I figured out the technology behind the idea, gave everyone instructions on how to use it, and served as the moderator for years.

As I look back, the trail is clear.

I love bringing people together, but not in just any way. I love seeing where people are not together and then creating an environment, a structure, or a program to bring them together.

It's no surprise that I'm involved in various areas of the women's ministry of my church and am always on the lookout for creative ways to bring women together for the betterment of the whole. Even when no one is looking for my help or suggestions, I can't help but offer them. I'm always thinking of innovative ways to create community.

Not only is it a natural gifting for me, being a gatherer of people is an ability I've cultivated over time, even without being aware of it. I am passionate about seeing people connect, and because personality tests tell me I'm a perfect balance between an extrovert and an introvert, I am suited for dealing with groups of people but am also a lover of one-on-one.

While I had no idea when I was having that identity crisis at age twelve and crying my eyeballs out in my parents' bedroom that creating community is what I'd one day be doing, it totally makes sense *now*. How did I get there? I followed the crumbs, discovered the knowledge of how God made me, and acted on the opportunities He provided.

Can I give you one more example of how to make peace with the Cheez-Its in your life?

My sister Priscilla teaches the Bible.

But what you may not know is that when she was in college, Priscilla worked at a radio station. And because of her familiar voice over the airwaves, someone asked her to lead a Bible study for a group of girls.

She didn't want to do it.

Leading a Bible study for a group of girls was not on her list of things to do. However, she loved God, loved the Bible, and loved to talk.

So she followed the breadcrumbs.

She decided it couldn't hurt to lead the study for a while and, well, you probably know how things ended up. (If you don't, just google "Priscilla Shirer.")

Do you see how this works?

First, you take the time to look at your life to see what is inside of you and who you already know yourself to be. Then you pay attention to the opportunities that come your way.

And then you act.

Maybe in small ways. Maybe in ways that may seem pointless. Maybe in ways that don't seem to have some grandiose finale. You choose to connect in the best way you know how based on who you are, how you're designed, and what experiences God has allowed on your path.

And then you act, willing to make connections in unexpected places or to walk through unexpected doors as God opens them on your behalf.

> Be willing to make connections in unexpected places or to walk through unexpected doors as God opens them on your behalf.

I know you may be thinking you don't have much to work with or you don't know enough to make an impact. But what if there's more than what you think you know? What if you only get to find out what you don't know by choosing to see, care for, and utilize the value that God has given you?

It's up to you to pay attention to and incorporate more of who you are into the life you have—on your job, in your home, within your community, and in your church. Your life's work is to discover and use your unique combination of gifts, abilities, interests, and nature—especially in the spaces and places that are life-giving for you.

> Connect what you know with what you do and watch new paths open up to you.

You may not know everything there is to know, but you don't have to!

Connect what you know with what you do and watch new paths open up to you.

Here's what I know.

God is sovereign. He always has a plan and destination in mind.

We just have to follow the crumbs.

Yellow or white cheddar.

Follow 'em.

Reflections for the Rescue

REMEMBER

You may not know everything there is to know, but you don't have to!

REFLECT

- What crumbs has God placed in you based on your design?
- What crumbs has God given you in His Word? Are you following them?
- What crumbs has God allowed in your experiences? What information do they give you?

RESPOND

Name one small step you can take based on the crumbs you notice in you, around you, or in God's Word.

———————————

Hebrews 13:20–21; Proverbs 16:9; Psalm 16:11; Psalm 25:4; Psalm 25:10; Proverbs 3:6; Zechariah 4:10; Psalm 119:133.

———————————

PART 3

EMBRACE
YOUR LIFE

Each of us has a fire in our hearts for something.
It's our goal in life to find it and keep it lit.

—*Mary Lou Retton*

To be yourself in a world that is constantly
trying to make you something else is
the greatest accomplishment.

—*Ralph Waldo Emerson*

CHAPTER 12

SLEEPING BY THE WINDOW

Nurturing Your Soul

For almost three years, I slept on the floor.

It's not that I didn't have a bed. I just preferred the space on the carpet next to it.

Back in my early twenties, I had a simple routine. Each night, I prepared a pallet on the floor with cushiony comforters and a few fluffy pillows at one end so I could lay down right in front of the bedroom window in my second-floor apartment.

Not too far away from that window was a pool that sparkled blue every evening. A small waterfall built from smooth stones sat on one end of the pool, and from the pallet where I lay I could hear the soothing sound of water trickling. I kept my window open and turned on the local jazz station—107.5 The Oasis.

With the melodies from the radio in one ear, the music from the flowing water in the other, and the breeze blowing against my face, I settled into my makeshift mattress and drifted off.

I slept like a baby.

When I woke up the next morning, I not only felt rested, but my soul also felt full. I felt alive and able to breathe. I'd done something simple to nurture *me* in a way that perfectly fit my soul.

And for a while each morning, it didn't even matter that I was headed to a job I didn't like.

Every evening I went to sleep to simple joys.

A view of water.

The sound of music.

And a touch of the outdoors.

During my early twenties, not only did I gain perspective on what to *do* based on the gifts God gave me, but I gained a new perspective on who I could *be*.

I grew to understand what filled up the cup of my soul and then overflowed into the rest of my life. Besides sleeping on that pallet, I made some other changes. I bought a bike, put a kid's seat on the back, and went out often for rides with my daughter. I joined the choir and started singing again. I reconnected with old friends and developed connections with new ones. I got reacquainted with the shape of me—the way God designed me, cracks, crevices, curves, and all.

I took the time to pay attention to the girl in me.

For many of us, our childhood offered us the gift of joy characterized and naturally infused by care of the soul.

We gazed out the windows, absorbing the sights and sounds of our worlds. We delighted in exploring the new and relishing the routine. And we got the recommended eight hours of sleep because our parents made us go to bed on time.

But alas, we all eventually move out of childhood.

I loved that window in my first apartment. But eventually I moved away.

Eventually, we all grow up.

For many of us, somewhere along the road from childhood to adulthood, we move away from the window that allowed us to nurture the girl inside. We become encumbered by responsibilities we have, jobs we must do, places we need to be, people we've invited into our space, and the distractions that interrupt our search for a new window that might give us the joy of real living.

We lose our innocence.

We stop laughing.

We work too hard and play too little.

And, if we're not careful, we forget what it means to simply *be*.

We exchange the important for the urgent—the nurture of our soul for the demands of the right now—and then wonder why we feel dry, empty, buried, or lost.

Well, at least that's how I felt.

I also didn't realize until many years later how much of myself I'd lost sight of because of slow drifts, unintentional decisions, and unexpected collisions. Life became full of have-tos and need-tos.

Doing consumed me. Being eluded me.

I've always known that God loves me, but looking back I realize that I often forgot He also gives me permission to love myself, embrace my life, and delight in simple joys.

And simple joys only enter through the windows that I take the time to open.

God didn't just create me; He created this wonderful world in which I live, and He intends for me to engage wholeheartedly with it, not neglecting to take care of my soul, which is the most important part of who I am.

> We exchange the nurture of our soul for the demands of the right now, and then wonder why we feel dry, empty, buried, or lost.

I forgot about the importance of cultivating joy—joy that can fill my soul in a world that daily drains it dry.

I forgot to keep looking for a window.

When I got pregnant as a teenager, I moved away from my window. Then I found it for a time when I remembered and rehearsed how much God loves me.

But then I forgot again.

When I found myself working jobs that drained me and didn't know what else my career might hold, I lost sight of my window. Eventually, I found it in a career that was challenging, fulfilling, and promising, but as soon as that job got stressful and unreasonably taxing, I lost sight of my window yet again.

Next came marriage, followed by more babies. Both were wonderful windows, but as much as I enjoyed cuddling my sweet children, I lost sight of my window the night I cleaned up the poop smudged into the carpet by one of those sweet but now stinky kids. I felt as if I were staring at a brick wall from behind bars while wearing heavy-duty handcuffs.

Nope. No window in sight that night.

As sleepless nights gave way to meal planning, making beds, schooling kids, and doing dishes, I lost sight of my window. Those short years ran across long days.

And then there was that time I went numb, gaining weight and packing on the pounds.

I've learned that my soul will not stay full on its own. Its filling takes my participation.

If there's one thing I know for sure, it's that this job of nurturing my soul is an ongoing labor of love—a love for the God who gave me that soul, and my willing effort to join Him in His love for the real me.

I've learned over the years, albeit slowly, what it means to look for simple joys, because God shaped me with a soul designed to hold them.

Simple joys didn't seem hard to find when I was a child chasing butterflies, turning cartwheels, and giggling uncontrollably. But you better believe my cooperation has been needed when studying for finals, fighting my way out of debt, or finding myself totally and utterly bored with my life.

Whether you are working two jobs, fighting infertility, or dealing with a devastating divorce, you still get to participate with God in caring for the real you.

So how do you go about filling up your soul?

What exactly does it look like to love yourself, embrace your life, and delight in simple joys?

I'm so glad you asked.

> **My soul will not stay full on its own. Its filling takes my participation.**

Your Senses

You were created with five senses—sight, smell, touch, taste, and hearing. Your physical body gives you a God-given way to perceive and experience your world.

You fill your soul when your eyes take in the words on the pages of a favorite book. You feast deeply on inspiration when you watch athletes at the top of their game, hear music that inspires, or touch the soft fur of a puppy.

I mean, doesn't something change in you immediately when you walk into Bath and Body Works and smell "spa"?

My mother has given me a good example of what it means to delight in simple joys in so many ways, but particularly via her senses.

My mother loves sunsets, so she makes time to watch them often. I see the joy in her face as she watches the sun go down, smiling because she feels the trickling of joy down deep within.

She loves flowers, and while my dad buys them for her often, my mother has been known to order them for herself, simply because they make her happy.

And my mom loves chocolate, as so many of us do. Cadbury Fruit and Nut, to be specific. When she decides to indulge, Hershey's won't cut it. She knows which stores carry her favorite and makes sure that those who love her know too.

When is the last time you engaged through your God-given senses something that caused you to smile, close your eyes with pleasure, or breathe deeply, taking it all in?

If you can't remember, it's probably been too long.

Your Significance

Much of the emotion we associate with our souls comes from our interactions with others. It's natural to want to know that we're significant in the estimation of other human beings. That we are seen and that we matter. That someone cares whether we are here, and that another person is a witness to our life.

Significance is a gift to be received.

Making time for 5:00 a.m. cups of coffee with friends has been a remedy for me during seasons when my days seem full. I have learned to communicate with those who care about me when I need their ear, their time, or both of their arms to squeeze me hard when the days are tough.

I've learned it's okay to have a healthy need for people who love, affirm, and care genuinely for the girl in me.

Relationships fill our cup—relationships with people who know us, value us, and treasure us.

And they should.

We were designed with connection in mind. God Himself exists in constant connection. He knows community—Father, Son, and Holy Spirit—and designed us in His image, so it's no wonder we desire the same.

We were created with a soul that needs to feel significant, and we need to share that significance with others. This is why it feels so good to give. When we validate another person's life through time spent, words spoken, or gifts shared, we benefit too.

Significance is a gift to be both given and received.

It's my great delight to send cards to people who cross my mind, or even a quick but heartfelt text message. I carry little sandwich baggies of care kits, made by my boys, so that when I see a person without a permanent home, I have something to give. And I give smiles. I've learned to smile when someone enters a room, because everyone needs to know that they are welcome, received, and noticed.

> Significance is a gift to be both given and received.

If you've let the busyness of life get in the way of the real business of life—letting yourself love and be loved—slow down and make some space.

The simple joy of significant relationships will spark a wonderful sense of satisfaction in your soul.

The Spirit

Now, before I sound like a free-spirited flower child who is out of touch with reality, let me assure you that I know what you're thinking.

Honey, I'm in a jacked-up place in my life, and you want me to grab some carnations from the grocery store?!

Well, yes, I do!

If that's what does it for ya.

But I also want to tell you that the joy that can fill your soul through your senses and significance is temporary.

That kind of joy doesn't last.

It can't.

We live in an imperfect world with rainy days and smelly diapers and eyes that grow dim with the passing of time.

We live in a world where people aren't perfect. They hurt us, betray us, and sometimes are too busy being themselves to notice us.

That's why your knowledge of who you are is so important. You are a soul in a body that is designed to be filled by the Spirit. At your core, you are a spiritual being, designed to have a spiritual experience. And that spiritual experience provides a path for joy that lasts.

My relationship with God and engagement with the Spirit in me are why I can have joy despite the chaos life might bring. But I also know what happens when I neglect disciplines that mark the well-lived spiritual life. I know from years of flowing in and out of consistent connection with God that keeping the connection is the only way my soul stays full and maintains its joy.

And the joy that God gives is not dependent on your being a Bible scholar. Resist pressure from people to look the part, say the right thing, or have it all together.

Your connection with the Spirit of God is the only experience that will give your soul access to an always-flowing source of joy.

Even if we don't have happiness, the Spirit offers us the gift of peace. Like my daddy says, "Peace doesn't mean you won't have problems. Peace means that your problems won't have you." While God calls us out of complacency, His peace allows us to choose contentment with our place in the world.

Know Spirit? Know peace.

No Spirit? No peace.

When you believe that you are loved by God and know the peace that He provides, you will know deep, abounding joy that is not dependent on your circumstances. Even in Galatians 5:22–23, joy makes its home between love and peace: "But the fruit of the Spirit is love, joy, peace, patience, kindness, goodness, faithfulness, gentleness, self-control; against such things there is no law" (NASB).

When you make room in your life for the Spirit, He offers to replace the joy and peace that slowly seeped out as you drifted away from your purpose, streamed out with your decision, or poured out from the impact of your collision.

I know, because He's done it for me over and over again.

My friend, just like you must cooperate by opening a window, buying a bunch of flowers, or engaging in conversations with friends along with your 5:00 a.m. coffee, you must cooperate by opening your Bible, making time for prayer, and walking in obedience.

I'm making an assumption here.

I'm assuming that you want to know God and that you want to experience His best in your life.

If you are an atheist, email me. We need to have a whole different conversation, which I'm totally open to having, by the way.

But if you feel you just aren't quite experiencing the fullness of God's Spirit in your soul or the steady filling of joy of which I speak, can I ask you a question?

How much time do you spend reading His love letter to you?

How much time do you spend talking to Him and sitting in quiet waiting for Him to speak to you?

How much attention do you pay to living a life that makes Him happy?

Relationships take time, and your relationship with God is no different.

I know you're busy, but make room for more of the filling of the Spirit in your life.

I know you're tired, but wake up a few minutes early to put His words in your heart.

> Relationships take time, and your relationship with God is no different.

I know you want what you want, but I dare you to go after what He wants for you and to watch your joy rise.

It's simple. Know Him, love Him, and seek to please Him, and you will know an unexplainable joy that simply overflows.

Choose to nurture your soul by cultivating joy.

Be conscious of paying attention to the joy available in all spheres of your life. Great care of your soul is not enough if you are neglecting significant relationships or the Spirit of God in you.

Choose joy by way of the senses, significance, and the Spirit.

Don't reach the end of your life or arrive at your goal and realize you were too focused on the result to enjoy the journey.

It's the path to your purpose that holds the real joy. If you want to live a life worth remembering, you must slow down and pay attention. It's the only way to see and appreciate all the beauty in and around you, and there is plenty of beauty to be seen in everyday life.

So I choose.

I choose to ride the amusement park rollercoasters with my kids in the dead heat of summer when my old and tired tail would rather be home in bed watching HGTV.

> Don't reach the end of your life or arrive at your goal and realize you were too focused on the result to enjoy the journey.

I choose to sit on my porch with some hot or cold tea, sweetened either way, and rock in silence by myself.

I choose to wake up every morning and stream music from one of my playlists that will set the tone for my day.

I choose to drink straight out of the milk container now and again for the sheer joy of doing it—and hope that my kids don't catch me.

I choose to spend time with those I love, looking them in the eye instead of staring at the device in my hand.

I choose to tell people I love them more often, and I choose to squeeze tight when someone reaches out to love me.

I choose to look for ways to give to others who can't return the favor, knowing that my gift to them is also a gift to me.

I choose to believe that God takes great delight in me and that He rejoices over me (Zeph. 3:17) and that his banner (and declaration) over me is love (Song of Sol. 2:4).

I choose to pause in the moments when I sense God's presence and just chat for a while without all the pomp and circumstance of a liturgical prayer.

I choose to make time for the study of His Word, to get to know Him better and to learn His principles for a well-lived life.

And I choose to trust Him with my life and believe that the joy that comes from Him gives me strength: "for the joy of the LORD is your strength" (Neh. 8:10 NASB).

While it is not my goal to reclaim all the joys I experienced in childhood, I get to choose each and every day to practice the art of living well in the season of life I am in. And when I cultivate the joy within my reach, even small joys grow and can begin to overflow.

I believe that if I can embrace the maturity and wisdom God has allowed me to gain from all my experiences—what I've learned about Him and the strength I've earned from diligent exercise of what I know to be true—I will live my life well.

I believe that you can choose too.

Even if it means choosing a spot on the floor, making yourself a pallet, and opening a window.

Reflections for the Rescue

REMEMBER

Choose to nurture your soul by cultivating joy.

REFLECT

- Simple joys matter. What can you engage in with your sight, smell, touch, taste, and hearing that will make you smile?
- Significant relationships matter. What person should you make time to talk to or be with? Give them a call or send them a text and plan a time to hang out.
- The Spirit of God gives joy. When will you make time to read His love letter to you and listen for His direction?

RESPOND

Make a list of things that nurture your soul and give you energy. Post the list in plain view. Refer to it often.

Zephaniah 3:17; Psalm 16:11; Jeremiah 31:13;
Ecclesiastes 9:7; Romans 15:13; Nehemiah 8:9–10;
Proverbs 17:22; Philippians 4:4; Psalm 30:5.

A LABOR OF LOVE

Finding Purpose in Your Pain

I'll never forget the moment when I gave birth to my first child and the doctor said, "It's a girl!"

Immediately I cried, "Oh, thank God—*it's out!*"

Before that moment, I had been in labor for fourteen hours, thinking I was going to die. Young and bullheaded, I'd told people that I would have my baby without drugs. In the moments when I felt like I was going to pass out from the pain, I kept thinking, "I have to follow through and do what I said I was gonna do!"

I recall a nurse coming in around 6:00 a.m. to check on me and, upon hearing my guttural groans, asking me if I wanted some meds to take the edge off the pain. When I told her I couldn't because I'd told everyone I would give birth without drugs, she said, "Well, honey, everybody ain't here right now!"

I still refused the drugs.

I lay on that bed, holding on to the side bar for dear life. My college roommate and lifetime friend gave me her hand to hold, bless her heart, but after a while she had to bow out and let me wrestle with the rail on my own.

She didn't want me to break her hand.

Hours later, as the clock approached noon and my mom and sister held my hands through the final agonizing stages of labor, I pushed through the pain, and my first child was born.

For just a second, the only thing I had on my mind was that the hard work of the labor was over and I was so grateful.

But then the doctor placed that sweet baby girl in my arms, and I was immediately smitten, and I've been smitten ever since.

I was finally able to see the girl who had been growing and developing inside me. But getting to her meant pressing through pain—some physical, some emotional. Some of the pain was self-inflicted. Some had been caused by another person. And some was simply a part of the process of giving life.

The pain had a purpose.

When you know your pain has a purpose, it changes your perspective.

Getting to the girl who is in you may require pressing through pain.

I've experienced all kinds of births, so I can testify to the fact that childbirth *will* hurt. I've done in-the-hospital-with-no-drugs, birth-at-home-with-a-midwife-and-a-birthing-tub, in-the-hospital-with-an-epidural, and a C-section.

It hurt each and every stinkin' time.

> When you know your pain has a purpose, it changes your perspective.

It doesn't matter how you give birth. It hurts before, during, and after. When you have to get a whole person to emerge from your own person, there is going to be some major discomfort involved.

The pain is a part of the process of bringing forth life.

And if we skip the pain, we skip part of the process.

I hate to tell you this, but your pain, however it came about, is a part of your journey. You don't have to want to relive, remember, or rejoice over it, but it *is* a part of who you are. Your pain affects how you see the world and therefore how you see yourself. It's a part of your experience, the stuff God has allowed to impact your soul.

So if you want to fully live your life, you must be willing to embrace your pain.

Your quest to rescue your life will require your labor of love.

Feeling Pain

I've learned that choosing to be awake in my life means knowing what joys fill my soul *and* being honest about what has impacted me—pain, suffering, hardship, and heartache.

Grief hurts, loneliness aches, heartbreak rips, disappointment deflates, and tragedy leaves a lasting impression.

But God can use it all if you will allow Him to. In the words of Rick Warren, "God wastes nothing."

However, you must be willing to give attention to your soul—both its current state and what may have happened previously to put it in the shape it's in.

Pressing through the pain is not the fun part of the birthing process, that's for sure, but it is a necessary one. If we try to push too fast past our pain, the injury that we've experienced can spread and can infect our head and our heart.

You have to stop and address it.

Look at it.

Acknowledge that you were—or are—hurt.

Cry over it.

Journal through it.

Read books that help you to navigate your experiences.

Find a support group.

Get counseling if you need it.

Know that it takes time to heal.

And be willing to *feel*.

During pregnancy and then while giving birth, I discovered parts of me that I didn't know I could feel. *After* giving birth, I remember holding my baby in my arms and being frustrated that even in this beautiful season of my life, my boobs hurt, my butt hurt, and I was exhausted from trying to keep up with the new life now in my care. With that first child, I had no idea that after the agony of natural childbirth, I'd have another set of hurdles to clear. Sitting in chairs required a donut cushion, going to the potty required me to grit my teeth, and I think I cried when I realized I had to do more than just pee.

Living, like having babies, involves pain.

And after the pain, there's a healing process.

Years later, after my C-section birth, I made the mistake of thinking I could get back to life faster because the doctors had sewn me up all nice and neat and handed me a bottle of painkillers on my way out the door. They urged me to take my time, rest, allow my body to heal.

You probably know by now that I'm a bit hardheaded and don't always listen to advice as well as I should.

Less than thirty-six hours after that birth, I got up, went into the kitchen to make breakfast, and bent over to grab a pan. My insides revolted. I thought I was going to pass out. Not paying attention to my pain, I'd created a different and deeper sort of ache.

Some of the worst things you can do—especially when you're excited to move to the next phase of the journey—are to move forward too fast, opt for temporary fixes, and not acknowledge the pain and how it affects you. If you don't give yourself time to heal, you can create weeks, months, or even years of damage to undo.

Sometimes the only way out is through.

Facing Pain

I'm sorry. I know that sucks to hear, especially if you are in a dark place right now, but I want to tell the truth. You've got to face your pain. It might not be fun to journey through the jacked-up places of your life, but it's only by traveling through the dark of night that you eventually run into your morning. "Weeping may endure for a night, but joy comes in the morning" (Ps. 30:5b NKJV).

The worst thing you can do when you've been hurt in a relationship is to move into another one too fast.

> Sometimes the only way out is through.

The worst thing you can do when you're disappointed about a promotion you didn't get or a transfer you were denied is to skip the process of growing where you are and instead rashly change your circumstances or give up out of frustration.

If you're up to your ears in debt, it does you no good to groan about the pressure of that situation without also being willing to adjust your thoughts and learn new habits that will enable you to move forward.

When you still feel the effects of the rape or molestation years after it's happened; when your children have broken your heart, even after all you've poured into them; when you're reeling from the news about your health; or when you're in a struggle with anxiety or depression, the worst thing you can do is pretend it doesn't hurt.

The infection will only fester and grow.

There's this one other funny thing that happens if you choose not to acknowledge and embrace your painful experiences in light of how God can use them.

You go numb.

When you cut off your ability to feel the pain, you also shortcut your ability to feel the joy.

While many faucets come with separate knobs for hot and cold water, the faucet in my kitchen sink has only one lever. Raising that lever and turning it to the left gives me hot water. Turning to the right gives me cold. But if I shut off the water by lowering the lever, I don't get either.

Your soul, like my faucet, can't be turned off to avoid one emotion and simultaneously be fully open to experiencing the other. As emotional creatures, both our joy and our pain help us to grow deep roots and live fully. If we choose the path of avoiding pain at all costs, we become apathetic creatures—people who have rejected our emotional makeup and would rather not care than feel anything at all.

> When you cut off your ability to feel the pain, you also shortcut your ability to feel the joy.

Persevering through your pain doesn't mean you have to like the process, but it does mean you need to trust that God can take your hurt and your heart and use them someway, somehow.

We typically do anything we can to avoid pain, but when we face our pain with the willingness to feel it, we open ourselves up to the very flow of our life.

Pain is information.

Finding Purpose

Physical pain is your body's way of telling you something isn't right and that you need to pay attention to the signals you receive and deal with the problem. Emotional, mental, and spiritual pain are signals too.

Pain is not the end of the road, though. It can be an opportunity.

The reason I choose authenticity and choose to tell you parts of my story is because it's from my pain that I've experienced what God can do in my life. I have been in the darkest of nights, afraid for my mind, my heart, and my life, wondering if anything good could come from my silent suffering, my hidden tears, or the deafening yet inaudible cries of my heart.

I know what it is to hide from yourself, to pretend the pain isn't real and to bite your lip to keep from crying at the wrong moment. I know what it is to feel the breaking of your heart and to be surprised when the sun actually does rise the morning after you cried yourself to sleep in the privacy of your pillow the night before. I have known my share of loneliness, rejection, embarrassment, grief, and betrayal.

But you know what? While the labor pain hurt me, it also helped me. It gave me a deep appreciation for my life, and then it birthed in me the desire to help you labor for yours.

In the words of Henri Nouwen, "Nobody escapes being wounded. We are all wounded people, whether physically, emotionally, mentally, or spiritually. The main question is not, 'How can we hide our wounds?' so we don't have to be embarrassed, but, 'How can we put our woundedness in the service of others?' When our wounds cease to be a source of shame, and become a source of healing, we have become wounded healers."[11]

I know from experience that pain has a purpose—a purpose for you and a purpose for others.

There are lots of great moms who love well because they knew what it was to feel unloved as a child.

Some of the best pregnancy-center counselors are women who went through the pain of their abortion alone.

Many great teachers are excellent educators because they remember how badly they struggled in school.

The best advocate for a woman who has survived abuse is one who herself has broken the cycle of living in abusive relationships and situations.

During your darkest moments, you may not see the victory waiting in your future. Functioning from one moment to the next might be all you can manage.

I know. I've been there.

During my dark moments, writing this book was not on my agenda. Functioning was. Moving from one minute to the next was all I could seem to manage. My focus was mental and emotional survival.

But, God.

I know what He can do.

And because I know what happens when you give God the fragments of your life, I share my life with you both to encourage and challenge you to walk through the pain and *feel*, exposing your head, heart, and hands to His healing power.

Yes. Do what you can to care for your soul. Do less. Say no. Make room for simple joys. Rest. Laugh. Play. Spend time connecting with God through reading His Word and talking to Him in prayer.

Yes. Get counseling—of the paid or the free varieties. Be brave enough to process your hard stuff with a trusted friend who is willing to listen and ask good questions. If you need more help than a friend can provide, call a church in the area or a professional. Don't be embarrassed. Get the help you need.

Yes. Join an accountability group. Find others who are willing to help you stay on track.

Yes. Journal. Purchase a pretty book and some colorful pens. Keep your appointment with yourself to cleanse your mind and process your emotions.

Yes. Go on a retreat. Rest matters.

Yes. Seek medical attention. Don't ignore what ails you. Call the doctor and take the test. Don't be afraid to seek healing.

Yes. Go to rehab. Whatever you have to sacrifice to make that work will be worth it.

Yes. Apologize for the pain you have caused someone else. Don't just feel sorry. Say you're sorry and make reparations if possible.

And then, once you've done all you can do, and with whatever you seem to have left, trust Him with the difference.

This is not an argument for making *unnecessary* mistakes or embracing unnecessary hardship. My aim is not to give you an excuse for poor decision-making, lack of discipline, or being ignorant of God's principles for living. Don't foolishly purpose to live a life that dishonors God and invite the pain that could have been avoided. Choose to learn and obey God's Word.

Stand on the promise that God can make a difference in your life and that Jesus died not only so you could one day live in heaven but also so you could experience a little bit of heaven right now. John 10:10 says, "I came that they may have life, and have it abundantly" (NASB).

Just because it hurt you doesn't mean it has to define you.

Your scars are real, but your healing can be too.

If you need help, get it.

But choose to persevere through your pain.

Feel it.

Face it.

But push through it, believing that God always has a plan and that His plan can make good use of your heartache, hardships, or mistakes.

Your pain is a part of the process that leads to the girl inside you living *her* life.

The pain that carves out pieces of your heart is the same pain that creates space in your soul to love with more compassion, live with greater wisdom, and experience an unexpectedly full, deep, and overwhelming joy.

> Just because it hurt you doesn't mean it has to define you.

Rescuing the girl in you means embracing all of you, even the painful parts.

Never forget that it's in the darkest of spaces and places that the light of God's hope can shine the brightest. He is a master of making miracles out of our messes.

Pressing through your pain is always a push for life.

And ultimately, that push for life is a labor of love.

Reflections for the Rescue

REMEMBER

Your pain has a purpose.

REFLECT

- Is there a painful experience from your past that you've not dealt with?
- How has pain served a purpose in your life? Has it helped you or made it possible for you to help someone else?
- If you are in a painful situation, do you need to ask for help? What might help you pay attention to the condition of your soul?

RESPOND

Going through a particularly rough time? Pray the words from Psalm 143 out loud.

James 5:13–16; Psalm 147:3;
Malachi 4:2; Matthew 11:28–29; Psalm 107:19–21;
Psalm 30:2; Romans 8:28; James 1:3; 2 Corinthians 12:9–10;
Romans 8:18; Revelation 21:4; 2 Corinthians 1:9–11.

ROCKIN' HOT CHOCOLATE

Do What You Can with What You Have

I didn't have much.

Just a full bed, a dresser, a small circular glass table with two cheap chairs, and a twenty-seven-inch JVC television.

And a rocking chair.

My first apartment, post-college, was 850 square feet. Two bedrooms and two bathrooms. I was on cloud nine to be in my own place with my little daughter.

Happy.

And broke.

My plan was to take my time saving money and slowly fill the place with a twin bed for my preschooler, a few furnishings, and a couch on which to sit and watch that twenty-seven-inch TV.

Since I only had that rocking chair, I bought a couple of large pillows so my girl could sit on a soft spot on the floor and watch Barney. (I wanted to shoot Barney. The "I Love You, You Love Me" song about drove me insane.) I sat in that rocking chair with my daughter sitting next to me on the pillows or dancing around the room to Barney songs, and made our odd little spot work until I could do something to improve it.

I had big plans for one day having a place where my social circle would come to hang out. I dreamed of the day when I had an area for everyone to sit and a spot for anyone who walked through my door to feel comfortable. I imagined hosting a slumber party for my daughter and visiting with the other mommies when they dropped off their girls for overnight fun. But I figured that all that would have to wait because I had nowhere for anyone to sit.

One day, though, I was talking to my aunt and sharing with her about my somedays. I told her about everything I planned to do *later*, after I'd made a little more progress in my life and could properly show hospitality.

She told me something I've never forgotten.

Do what you can with what you have.

Don't wait for the day when you have the right couch, coffee table, or seating arrangement. Don't wait until you have an eating area for a sizable dinner party. Don't delay making memories or sharing your life with your friends.

Do what you can to live your life well with what you have.

I was reminded of this memory recently when a friend and I were reminiscing on the good old days. (Wait, am I old enough to have good-old-days kinds of memories? Lawd, help!) My girlfriend reminded me how she'd come over to that apartment—the one with only one rocking chair—and I'd make us hot chocolate topped with swirls of whipped cream. We would sit together—me on the floor and her in the rocking chair—sipping away, having great conversations and developing a friendship we still enjoy today.

> Do what you can to live your life well with what you have.

Even though it seemed like I didn't have much to work with, I decided to follow my aunt's advice and live my life regardless of whether I thought

I had much to live it with. I'd always known from reading my Bible that contentment is important. I chose in this season to live like I believed it.

Listen, I know that as I've talked to you about gaining a new perspective, living with a satisfied soul, and pushing through the pain, you might not think you have much to work with. I wish that right now I could put my hands on your shoulders and look you in the eyes with a smile to tell you this important secret to coaxing your girl out of her corner.

Do what you can with what you have.

Your job is to live well, embracing what you do know, what you can do, and who you can be—today. If you wait until you have enough information or ability, the perfect opportunity or circumstances, or exactly the right mood, mindset, or physical makeup, you're pushing pause on your life.

Even if you choose to stop living, the clock does not stop ticking.

As a person who has pushed pause on her life—more than once, I might add—I get why we tend to do this.

We're tempted to wait until just the right moment to do the right thing or a "big" thing. And while we wait, we do "no" thing. We want to wait until we've reached the perfect age or have the perfect relationship. We want to wait until we feel brave enough, strong enough, good enough, or motivated enough. We want to wait until someone gives us the opportunity or notices we're standing there waiting for them to notice us. We wait because we feel afraid, hopeless, unsure, or unimportant.

And while we wait on just the right moment to care for our souls, deal with our pain, or change our outlook, life can pass us by.

But never forget, you have the ability to choose. Each and every day, you can choose to do something that honors the girl inside you.

Choose to see what God has placed inside you to give to the world, and look for ways to use those attributes.

Choose to value the power of a satisfied soul enough to pour in what brings life to you and offer that life to others from your abundant overflow.

Choose to face your pain and acknowledge your hard places. Refuse to ignore the hurt or the ache and, instead, actively seek healing, trusting that your pain can be a gift to your present.

You don't honor your girl by passively leaving the door open, letting time pass, and hoping that she might one day walk through it.

You search for her.

You call her out.

During my college years, "doing what I can" sometimes looked like getting out of bed in the morning and making it through the day without running to the bathroom to catch the flood of tears. In this season, I learned that if doing one basic thing to survive is all I can do, that's enough.

In my twenties, "doing what I can" was rediscovering the value God had given me and using my gifts in small ways here and there. In this season, I learned that God wastes nothing—even the random, seemingly disconnected segments of my life.

During my thirties, "doing what I can" involved fighting to find joy in mundane days of changing diapers, not getting a paycheck, doing dishes, and finding a gazillion ways to fix chicken. In this season, I learned the art of cultivating my own soul.

And my forties? "Doing what I can" has meant being honest about the pain of my past, unlearning the skill of being numb, and opening myself up to the beauty of authenticity and transparency. In this season, I'm learning that the girl I lost somewhere along the way has been there all along, waiting for me to do the work of finding her.

That's why I'm so passionate about helping you do the same thing.

It starts with doing what you can with what you have to work with *today*, and trusting that over time it will make a difference.

You encourage the girl in you to make use of her one rocking chair, even if she doesn't think it amounts to much. Because one day, she might look back and see that there was so much value in using what she had and doing the small thing that was within her reach, capability, and bandwidth.

You just never know what can come tomorrow from doing what you can do today.

Sometimes it's as simple as embracing what brings you joy and fills your soul.

I've always wondered how Mother Teresa became Mother Teresa—a woman renowned worldwide for taking care of others.

After all the accolades and attention, the bottom line is that Mother Teresa loved on people. She knew that serving the needy filled her soul, and she faithfully allowed her life to overflow to others. She didn't start with fame or notoriety. She didn't wait until she had just the right set of circumstances, the ideal amount of money, or a certain number of people paying attention. She simply honored the love in her heart and the call on her life and embraced the opportunities she had to make a difference as she could.

> You just never know what can come tomorrow from doing what you can do today.

Sometimes doing what you can involves pushing through pain.

Almost fifty years ago, Joni Eareckson Tada became a paraplegic after diving into a lake and severing her spinal cord. She has not had use of her legs or arms since she was a teenager. During the darkest times of her life and seasons of great physical and emotional pain, she decided to rediscover her love of art and figure out how to once again participate in a creative experience. Joni learned how to paint by holding a paintbrush with her mouth. Her artwork began selling, and this inspired her to do more with her life.

Many people know about Joni because, ten years after her accident, she wrote her own autobiography, sharing the story of her difficult journey. A few years later, that story became a movie. For many years, Joni has used that platform to champion the cause of the physically disabled and tell people about her love for God.

But ultimately, Joni really focused on doing what she could with what she had. She had a creative spirit. She had a mouth. She had a paintbrush.

Maya Angelou had a painful past and a pen. She did what she could with what she had and is now remembered as a brilliant poet who gave words to thousands of people who make sense of their experiences through her writings.

Sometimes doing what you can opens doors that you never could have imagined.

As Sara Blakely sold fax machines door to door, becoming an entrepreneur was the last thing on her mind. But one day, she cut the feet off her pantyhose and wore the cropped hose underneath her pants to smooth out her panty lines.[12]

Voila! Spanx was born. Aren't we all grateful she reached for those scissors?

Doing the best you can with what you have has a funny way of giving birth to surprising new paths and perspectives. In fact, God proves over and over in the Scriptures that He loves to use people who are willing to do what they can with what they have.

When Moses questioned God's call on his life, God asked Moses to use what he had—a common stick used to guide sheep—to deliver half a million people out of Israel (Exod. 4:1–5).

> God proves over and over in the Scriptures that He loves to use people who are willing to do what they can with what they have.

When as a young man David experienced a burning passion to defend God's glory, God enabled him to do what a whole army was unwilling to do. David faced a giant and knocked him out with what he had—a pebble and a slingshot (1 Sam. 17:22–40).

When Jesus and His disciples were discussing solutions for feeding five thousand hungry people, a little boy allowed the disciples to have his five fish and two loaves of bread. He was willing to use what he had, make his next meal available for God's use, and believe that Jesus could do something with what little he had to give (John 6:8–10).

God not only invites you to do what you can with what you have, He *requires* you to do so. In order for you to experience the fullness of what He can do in and through your life, He calls for you to engage in your life.

In Matthew 25:14–30, Jesus tells the story of a man who entrusted different levels of wealth in the form of talents to three of his servants before he planned to be absent for a time. Upon his return, the man asked for an account of those assets. He expected that while he was away, the servants would use what they had to return more to him than they'd received.

The servant who had received five talents doubled his investment and now had ten. The servant who had been given two talents doubled his investment and now had four. But the man who'd been given one talent did nothing with what he had. Afraid he would bumble the job, he simply sat around and waited. And his master showed no sympathy for the servant's reasoning to play it safe and hope for the best. Instead, he chided him for his failure to try.

When you choose to do what you can with what you have, you move from waiting on your girl to walk through the door to inviting her to come in.

It may seem as if you have a lot of work to do to get to the girl in you. But don't be overwhelmed by what you don't know. Don't get bogged down by what you can or can't do right now. You don't have to have the perfect perspective, feel completely satisfied in your soul, or be totally past your pain.

You only need to be faithful to do what you can with what you have and what you know right now.

Maybe you can't afford canvas or an art class, but what if you use your pencil and draw regularly in your sketchbook?

Maybe you can't quit your day job to write full-time, but could you commit to putting words on paper three hours a week?

Maybe you can't afford the four-year degree, but how about starting with one class at the community college?

The debt may seem insurmountable, but what if you tackle it bit by bit, one bill at a time?

It may seem impossible to carve out any time for what fills you, but what about starting with five minutes, hiding from your kids in the bathroom for a bit of peace and quiet while pretending to go potty?

The clutter could be crowding you out of your own home, but can you set a timer for fifteen minutes each day to conquer one corner, one box, or one stack?

The loneliness may seem overwhelming, but are you able to fight back by inviting a new friend over for coffee and dessert?

Choose every day to wake up and find one thing you *can* do to honor the beautiful being you are and the beautiful life only you can live. Before you know it, you'll see the girl in you coming out of the shadows.

Who knows? She might even join you for hot chocolate and whipped cream in the rocking chair.

Reflections for the Rescue

REMEMBER

You never know what can come tomorrow from doing what you can do today.

REFLECT

- What are you pushing pause on in your life?
- Do you feel like God can use you? Why or why not?
- What actions or opportunities are in front of you? Are you acting on them? Why or why not?

RESPOND

Don't focus on what you can't do. Think about what is possible. What does "doing what you can" look like right now? Make a list of actions you can take right now, big or small. Remember, you can always do *something*.

Exodus 3:1–14; 4:1–17; Judges 7:2–8; 1 Peter 4:10–11;
1 Timothy 4:14; Luke 16:11; Matthew 25:14–30;
Colossians 3:23–25; Proverbs 18:16; Colossians 3:17.

CHAPTER 15

AN ANSWER, NOT *THE* ANSWER

The Process of Your Progress

I have a friend named Shelly. We've been friends since my senior year in high school. Shelly graduated a year before me, and while she did go on to college, she didn't have a particular passion in her heart to work toward. Not only that, she wasn't confident she could be successful in school. She didn't think she was smart enough.

Finishing didn't come easy. She took classes on and off, stopping when she didn't have either the money or the motivation to keep going.

She was frustrated because she didn't know *the* answer—the *what* she wanted to do and the *why* she wanted to do it. Working toward her undergraduate diploma seemed pointless if she didn't know how she was going to use it.

Between graduating from high school and receiving her undergraduate diploma ten years later, Shelly worked a wide variety of jobs that spanned multiple industries, cities, and levels. Shelly loved change. She cleaned hotel rooms and worked the cash register at Whole Foods Market. She made desserts in the back of a bakery and worked in customer service at a nonprofit organization. She loved people. She assisted in production on a cooking show in one state and unloaded merchandise at Banana Republic on the night shift in another. Shelly loved to travel.

In her late twenties, Shelly simply got tired of going to school. Partly out of exasperation and partly out of a need to finish something she'd started, she made up her mind to focus on completing her post-high-school education.

Shelly figured that she would have more opportunities available to her if she simply completed some degree, any degree. She looked at her options for earning a diploma, picked the degree plan that would help her finish the fastest, and made up her mind to work toward that end. She successfully earned her degree by the time she was thirty.

Finishing school wasn't *the* answer, but it was *an* answer that moved her forward.

With her degree in hand, Shelly decided it was time for *an*other answer—a job that paid more based on her having a four-year degree.

After looking in the paper and online, Shelly found a position working at the front desk of a cardiologist's office. Eventually that office closed, but she'd made a connection with another medical professional at a gastroenterologist's office. At some point on that job, she noticed she was curious about working in the medical field long-term. A few years later, a friend who worked in the NICU at a local hospital told Shelly about a job opening there. This presented *an* answer to Shelly's prayers for a new level of responsibility in a field she was growing to love. Shelly interviewed, applied for, and got the job.

While working in the NICU, Shelly became friends with an ER tech who encouraged her to think about becoming a nurse, something Shelly had wondered about as a teenager but didn't think she was smart enough to do.

At this point, *an* answer was more than the next job; it was the beginning of her career. Shelly was now motivated to go back to school for a two-year nursing degree.

Shelly is now a full-time nurse who travels from city to city working at different hospitals for contracted periods. She gets to travel, experience change, and love on people every day. She has earned a four-year degree in nursing. She loves her job. She loves her life. Never would Shelly have thought she could love her job *and* the life it gives her, but because she was willing to go from *an* answer to *an*other answer, she discovered *the* answer to what she should do for a living. And Shelly just told me she's considering graduate school.

While she often had no idea what *the* answer would be, Shelly learned the beauty of being patient with the process of progress in her life.

There's a common problem many of us will face in our lifetime. Because we want to live fully and know we've given our best shot at our one opportunity to walk this earth, we want to know *the* answer for how best to make that happen.

For some of us, *the* answer seems to elude us.

And looking for *the* answer stresses us out.

We tend to glorify people who seem to have it all figured out. They appear to know exactly where they're headed and how they'll go about getting there. As for the rest of us, well, not knowing *the* answer might make us feel a little challenged, like something is wrong or maybe we were sleeping when God was handing out passion and purpose.

It can be frustrating to want to honor your girl by living a life she will be proud of but not knowing exactly how to make that happen.

Well, let me take some of the pressure off you.

Your job is not to find *the* answer that leads to a master plan or purpose. Your job is to move forward as you become aware of *an* answer you can act on. You must accept that *an* answer is part of the process to getting to *the* answer.

When you choose to do what you can with what you have, you are taking a step into a process of living. Your ability to honor the girl who lives in you will involve your willingness to accept that the one thing you can do today is a part of your progress, even if that progress doesn't look anything like *the* answer you hoped to find.

Part of loving your life is learning to be content, appreciating each step you take, and believing that even *an* answer is good enough for right now.

Your answer for today can lead you to *the* answer for tomorrow.

Remember how we talked about your unique design and your unique experiences? You have gifts, abilities, interests, and a nature that are the precious cargo you have been given to carry.

> Part of loving your life is learning to be content and appreciating each step you take.

When you are looking to acknowledge *an* answer, you start by looking at what's already inside you and what you already have access to in the way of experiences and opportunities. Then you simply decide to be a good steward of your gifts.

Build on the gifts God gave you. Don't minimize them or mistakenly perceive them as small or insignificant. This is an error many of us make, and make often. We diminish the things we have been endowed with, then wonder why *the* answers do not rise up to greet us. Everything that has been deposited in you and all that you have experienced can be built on. God has already given or allowed the raw material you need to build a life worth living. You just have to be a good steward of the gift.

While I've shared with you how I noticed the breadcrumbs God put in my path, what I didn't tell you was that I've spent a lot of time being a whiny brat when the breadcrumbs didn't seem to present themselves fast enough or take me where I thought I wanted to go.

I didn't understand that the seemingly insignificant answers were part of the process of my progress. However, over time I've gained new perspective. When we act on *an* answer, using what God has given us and using it well, we honor our process and give God something to work with.

I've heard my father say a million times, "God loves to hit a moving target." It's true. We are more apt to find *the* answer when we're willing to move on with what we can know and do today. And how exactly do you move forward? You practice who you are and what you love. By moving on with the answers available to you, you will also be moving toward more answers that are waiting to be discovered.

Build on the gifts God gave you. Don't minimize them.

Misty Copeland, the first African-American female principal dancer with the American Ballet Theatre, didn't grow up dreaming about being a professional ballerina. She grew up in a single-parent home where there wasn't really extra money for dance lessons.

But Misty did know she loved to dance, so she joined the drill team at her school. The team coach noticed her natural ability and recommended she take ballet at the local Boys and Girls Club. Misty's gift continued to open doors for her as she discovered a growing passion for a direction in her life she didn't even know was possible.[13]

Recognize what God has put in you. Notice what brings you joy and satisfies your soul. Acknowledge your experiences, recognize your pain, and see all that has been allowed into your life as the stuff that can fill your soul, but not define it. Then move toward *an* answer—some answer—and trust that doing so enters you into a process of engaging with the girl only you can be.

I'm virtually positive that Celine Dion loves doing what she does for a living. Oprah probably does too. I grew up watching Janet Jackson dancing on stage, moving her hips in ways I couldn't fathom doing with my own. She loves dancing and it shows. Who wouldn't want to spend their lives doing something they love, something that seems to be *the* answer for their lives?

Many of us spend a lot of time looking at people who have widely recognized gifts, talents, or experiences, and we wish we had the answers they've been able to find. We see their product but don't value their process. If we did, we'd more highly value our own. We don't value what we love as answers worth celebrating, working at, cultivating, and

> Practice who you are and what you love.

appreciating. If we did, we might realize we're just as much in love with our lives as we imagine others to be in love with theirs, even if our hips won't move in the ways we wish them to.

Celebrities aren't the only ones who find the answers, remember? *Anyone* who is faithful to the process of their progress can live fully. We all do it the same way—*an* answer at a time.

My aunt, whom we lovingly call Auntie, has always loved children. She's never been married and never had children of her own, yet she has made time for other people's children often. She didn't just babysit; she served and ministered to children at church. She even provided a home for one of her nieces every summer so that her mom, my aunt's sister, could have a break. She spent time doing more of what she knew she loved, and that provided *an* answer in her life.

Did she want to be married at one time? Yes.

Did she want her own children? Yes.

But she didn't let her circumstances stop her from operating in *an* answer available to her.

Today Auntie has her doctorate in education. She has served as the director of our children's ministry at church. And she still makes time to let her great nephews and nieces—including my own children—spend the night in her home (thank you, Jesus). The beautiful thing about my aunt is that she has lived her life practicing who she is and what she loves, even when she didn't know what that love would lead her to do. And Auntie would tell you that as much of an accomplishment as her PhD is, it does not trump the joy she's experienced throughout her life being faithful to the process of her progress.

Grandma, my maternal grandmother, was eighty-one years old when she was presented with an honorary associate of arts degree from a community college. She had earned enough credit hours for a degree, but her studies over the years weren't directed in any specific area. As a woman who didn't begin her higher education until she was fifty-five, she had to start and stop again to flex with the needs of her family. But because she loved learning, she kept going back, taking classes—riding the bus when necessary to get there—and racking up the hours over the years.

When my sister learned that Grandma had been in school for more than twenty-five years without earning a degree, she went to the dean and asked if something could be done to celebrate her lifelong heart for learning. The honorary associate of arts was the answer to that request.

But it wasn't *the* answer for my grandmother.

The answer for Grandma was that her eight children saw her love of learning. Because of her sacrifices—working three jobs, moving from her home country in South America, and taking breaks from her own education to make sure her children got theirs—*the* answer was a love of learning and a love for God she was able to instill in her children.

When you practice who you are and what you love, you leave a mark on your world and on the people within your sphere of influence. When you leave this world, you will know you have lived fully, and others will know you were here.

Building on the gift God has given you means practicing who you are and what you love. You may be practicing for a while as you wait on God for guidance, direction, or an answer. But the practice and the wait are worth it.

Trust that as you embrace your life by doing what you can with what you have, *an* answer today will be a part of the process for *the* answer tomorrow.

And because God made you in His image, the more you seek Him as the ultimate answer, the more you will find out about yourself and the answers you seek for your life.

Reflections for the Rescue

REMEMBER

Build on the gifts God gave you.

REFLECT

- What can you do to build on the gifts God has given you?
- Are you making room to do things that you love? Why or why not?
- What is *an* answer you can take action on today?
- What small step can you take to steward the gifts God has given you?

RESPOND

Since you are the steward of the gifts, abilities, interests, and nature God has given you, what small step can you take today to build on what you've been given? Consider what you can do to develop the gift of you.

Philippians 3:13–14; Matthew 25:14–30;
Mark 12:41–44; Luke 16:10; Psalm 90:12.

PART 4

DEVELOP YOUR LIFE

To pay attention, this is our endless and proper work.

—*Mary Oliver*

Yes, you may feel unqualified, uneducated, untrained, under-gifted, or even unworthy. Yet, those are excellent qualifications for God to do a mighty work.

—*Chuck Swindoll*

DIG DEEP

Focus on the Finish

M y youngest son is an athlete at heart. When I call out a fifteen-minute warning before we jump in the car to head for some kind of sports practice, he lights up with excitement and scurries around gathering all of his equipment so we'll be ready to roll.

As I write this chapter, we're in the middle of track season. This little boy runs every race hard. He frequently leaves the asphalt in tears, heaving like he's in serious need of Albuterol because every drop of energy has gone to running his race. His most recent 400-meter relay was no different.

When my son extended his arm behind him to receive the baton from his teammate, they were in fourth place. This son of mine hates— and I mean *hates*—to lose. So he sprinted out in his lane fast. Too fast. Watching from the sidelines, I saw how much energy he was expending trying to close the distance between himself and the three teams in front of him.

He did it too.

He quickly passed the guy in third. He zoomed past the guy in second. And before the first 100-meter curve was complete, he had moved in front of the little guy in first place. He held that first place position for the second 100 meters. But somewhere around the 200-meter mark, his energy waned, his legs started "talking to him," and he began to slow down.

He was exhausted after having spent so much energy catching up. During the third 100 meters, he fell from first to second, and it appeared he would soon fade back to third. But right at the moment when the next runner was about to catch him, he heard a familiar voice.

My husband was waiting for him at the start of the last 100 meters. He was shouting out to our little runner that he was almost at the finish line. "Focus on the finish, son! You are almost there! Dig deep! Focus on the finish!" Between the sound of my husband's voice and the breath of the boy in third place on the back of his neck, my son found a source of strength. The look on his face changed from numb exhaustion to a grimace of agony and determination. His legs started moving faster and his arms started pumping harder as he pushed through to the end of his race.

"Look at him!" I thought, motherly pride welling up in my heart. "He's giving it all he's got."

Something changes when you focus on the finish.

Something shifts when you put your energy to work in a specific area of your life and do what it takes to move forward.

> Something changes when you focus on the finish.

Something happens when you dig deep and keep a clear view of where you're going no matter how distant or blurry and unclear that finish line might seem.

I'm not going to lie to you. I struggle with focus. Not long after I decide to make healthier choices with food, there always seems to be some event where something salty or sugary is calling my name. Right after I decide to start reading one book, another pops up to vie for my attention. As soon as I start looking up something I need to know on my phone, I find myself distracted by a notification that entices me away from the task at hand.

There is no doubt about it. Living with focus can be hard.

I have people in my life who do a good job of living with focus, and I can see the blessings that hail from their choice to live this way. My brother Anthony is one of those people.

Anthony is a singer and songwriter who has worked in the music industry for years doing what he loves. Recently, he started an entertainment company that produces shows, tours, and events of all sizes.

I can clearly remember my baby brother singing in the choir on Sunday mornings at church. I'm filled with amazement to see what time invested in his God-given talents has produced. Watching him all those years ago, entertainment company ownership wasn't even a thought in my mind. So I asked him recently about focus—how he's developed it and how he's kept it.

First, Anthony told me that focus always starts with a simple decision to do one thing with what you have. My brother had a decent voice, so he decided to sing in the church choir.

Second, he decided on a direction. More than simply singing here and there as he had a chance to, he followed the breadcrumbs God placed in his path. He auditioned for a singing group in college. He sang backup for other artists for years. He figured out what it took to create his own album, then repeated that work to create more albums.

Third, he used discernment. He kept people around him who encouraged him in his focus. He sought out resources to learn about the direction he'd chosen, and he put himself in environments that gave him great opportunities to grow.

Finally, he exercised discipline. It wasn't easy to write songs when he didn't feel like writing. He sometimes missed out on opportunities to hang out with friends when it was time to record in the studio. He invested money in his projects when he might have bought a new car, taken a trip, or moved into a bigger apartment. But he willingly did the hard things that his passion presented to him as opportunities for excellence and growth.

> Focused living always starts with a simple decision to do one thing with what you have.

He started by doing the one thing he knew to do, and then he focused on doing it well.

He kept choosing to focus on the finish line. One race at a time.

If you're like me, you may look at others who seem focused and think they must have something you don't have or know something you don't know.

But there is not some huge secret to finding the girl who has been lost in the shadows and bringing her out of hiding. We just have to focus enough of our time and energy on the task at hand.

Lest you think this idea of focus only applies to certain kinds of people, let me tell you what focus has looked like in my life—you know, in an everyday-girl kind of way.

People always ask me how was I able to make it through school with a baby in tow. I've thought long and hard about that, wondering what I did that was so phenomenal. And I'm convinced it wasn't anything exceptional at all. I simply had the desire to dig deep and finish something I'd started that was worth my time and effort.

Maybe, at the beginning, I was naive enough to think it wouldn't be that hard. Maybe I was motivated by the need to support myself and my new baby girl. Maybe I was like my son and simply didn't want to quit.

Whatever the rationale was, the bottom line is that I made a decision.

For most of us, keeping our eyes focused on the finish line isn't about winning a medal. It's about turning in papers and taking tests for four years. It's about honoring the appointment on our calendar to work out with a friend. It's about taking a risk to audition for a local theater production. It's about choosing to return to the volunteer work that lit our hearts on fire as teens. It's about digging deep to put one foot in front of the other on our way to the finish line.

That season of my life required discipline. When my friends were out partying on Friday nights, I was home studying. It also required discernment. I became adept at nurturing relationships that were encouraging and life-giving to me during one of the hardest seasons of my life. When I did have time to read, I chose books about time management and motherhood. During this season that required me to focus and dig deep, I didn't have the time or energy to entertain just any old thing or any old body.

This was a pattern I'd need to repeat a decade later.

When my husband and I got married, we both had high-commitment jobs. He traveled a lot and would be gone for days or weeks at a time. By this time, my job was also fairly demanding, and we were both feeling the tug on our time with each other. We each brought a daughter into our marriage, and we felt the tug on our blended family too. We decided that at least one of us should be able to have the time to look the girls in the face.

I resigned from my job.

For the next ten years, I was a stay-at-home mom. Because of my husband's travel for work, I often operated like a single parent. As much as I love my girls, the three boys who came along after them, and the season spent making a home for us all, being a full-time mom and homemaker ain't for punks. It's the hardest but most worthwhile thing I have done or ever will do, but it's h-a-r-d. I gave up my job, my title, my regular lattes, and my paycheck to wipe bottoms, watch Barney, and eventually homeschool our artsy oldest daughter, who was struggling in school.

It takes discipline to serve others, particularly when they don't say thank you or pat you on the back for a job well done. It takes willpower to stay up late and get up early. You have to dig deep to do the dishes again when you just did them a few hours before. But in this season, I learned the beauty of discernment. I found my tribe with other moms online, in person, or on the bookshelf.

During that leg of my race, I was focused on the finish—the goal of raising children who love God wholeheartedly, love others generously, and love themselves as well.

While I'm still on that journey, I've also started others that require my focus.

In the last five years of my life, I've had other reasons to dig deep. I chose to start writing and speaking. I decided to love my husband well during a season of illness. I purposed to do a better job taking care of the body that houses my spirit and soul.

I want my choices to move me in the direction of my goals—using my gifts, honoring my marriage vows, and stewarding my health. Those decisions require discipline, sometimes more than I think I have. They also require discernment to know which people or resources can support me and how much I can engage with them.

Every single one of these areas requires focus.

You will have to dig deep to make decisions that are sometimes hard in order to head in a direction that sometimes seem scary, to exercise discipline that doesn't always feel good, and to use discernment to operate in an environment that can keep you from your focus.

And you will have to say no—often. So practice saying no. Even if you have to say it to a tree. Get good at it. If you don't say no, I can guarantee that the urgent in your life will always eclipse the important.

I don't know what digging deep will look like in your life, with the decisions that you must make to honor the life of the girl in you, but I do know that you will have to focus to do it.

There is no other way.

The good thing about focus is that it's available to anyone, anywhere.

Every daughter who goes with her mother, aunt, or friend to chemo appointments is digging deep. Every woman who faces the glass ceiling on her job but keeps doing excellent work with less pay is operating with focus. Every mom who does whatever it takes to care for aging parents while balancing her own family and job is doing the hard work of pressing toward her finish line while serving others well.

> Practice saying no. Even if you have to say it to a tree. Get good at it.

And every woman who makes time to care for her soul by being still, getting rest, cultivating joy, and living with a healed whole heart, especially when constant demands on her time make it difficult to do, is doing today what will move her toward some finish line tomorrow.

It doesn't matter if you haven't lived a focused life up to this point. Start today. The apostle Paul says, "Brethren, I do not regard myself as having laid hold of it yet; but one thing I do: forgetting what lies behind and reaching forward to what lies ahead" (Phil. 3:13 NASB).

Choose to dig deep.

Choose to live with focus.

And I promise you that the more you do, the clearer you will see the finish line as you move toward it.

Reflections for the Rescue

REMEMBER

Dig deep and focus on the finish.

REFLECT

- What hinders you from staying focused?
- What is the hardest part of focus for you? Making the decision, picking a direction, using discernment, or exercising discipline? How could you work on that?
- In what area of your life is focus most needed?

RESPOND

Identify one thing you need to say no to so that you can say yes to the things that matter most.

Hebrews 12:1–2; 1 Corinthians 9:24–27;
2 Timothy 4:7; Galatians 5:7; Proverbs 4:25–27.

CHAPTER

17

ANALYSIS PARALYSIS

Make a Decision

A nyone who knows me well knows I can be *extremely* indecisive. Because I have perfectionist tendencies, I don't like making mistakes. I don't like doing things wrong, and I don't like having regrets. This means that I take *forever* to make a decision because I want the decision I make to be the right one.

Let me give you an example.

I went with my daughter and her husband to Philadelphia as their "nanny" for a weekend while they traveled out of town for work. (Yes, I'm a grandmother. Don't know how that happened, because as far as I'm concerned, I'm still twenty-seven.)

My dad is from Baltimore, Maryland, and my grandfather—the last living grandparent I have—still lives there. In the middle of my trip to Philly, I decided to make the two-hour trip to Baltimore to see my grandfather.

I had two options. I could rent a car and have control over my schedule, or take the train and enjoy the ride. Simple enough, right?

I decided to take the train. My spontaneous decision meant I hadn't

177

checked the train schedule, so on the cab ride to the station, I checked the website and realized the next train left in fifteen minutes. I was ten minutes away. Realizing that my chances of catching that train were beyond slim, I changed my mind and decided to rent a car.

I asked the cab driver to take me to the car rental agency. As we made our way through traffic and drew near our destination, I realized that the rental agency was only one block from the hotel where the driver had not long before picked me up. *Ugh.*

I walked into the agency, stood at the counter, and waited for the representative to help me find a cheap economy car. When she found it, the price was much higher than I'd expected. I checked the time for the next train and noted that the cost would be about the same as the car rental. So I thanked the rental rep for her assistance, declined the car, then went outside to find yet another cab.

At the train station, I found my way to the ticket booth, decision made. Or so I thought. When the agent in the booth quoted me the price of the train ticket, it was twice as high as I'd expected it to be. That would be because I hadn't looked at the round-trip price—only the one-way.

Brilliant, Chrystal.

So you know what I did?

Yup. Mmm hmm. You guessed it.

I went back to the car rental agency.

While I eventually did get in the car and get on my way, my indecisiveness had cost me something precious—time with my grandfather, the very focus of the trip I was trying to take.

Sometimes the best decision you can make is simply to make a decision.

Making a decision seems simple enough, doesn't it? You have at least two choices and then you pick one, right?

Yeah, right.

If that were the case, then the road of life wouldn't be marked with flat squirrels who couldn't make a decision.

Analysis paralysis is real. I know this all too well. I can't tell you how many times I've delayed some decision or never decided at all because I was overwhelmed by overthinking the options. For me, the decision to make some changes in my hair-care regimen can result in a three-hour field trip to Target trying to determine just the right products to bring home.

I remember the time I couldn't decide on which fitness tracker to buy, so I bought three of them. And then I wore them all simultaneously for a week to see which one was more accurate, had the better phone app, and gave me the most data on my daily activities.

By the end of the week, I was so confused that I took them all back.

I would have been better off just closing my eyes, picking one, then going home and using it.

The problem for most of us is not making a decision, it's making a decision that results in action. Yet results come only when we take action. We have to move from thinking about it to doing something about it. Wanting to honor the girl in you is admirable, but until you're willing to participate in that process, nothing will happen, and that's the part of decision making where most of us get tripped up and off track.

I love helping others make decisions, probably because I know how much help I need in making them. When I realize that someone I know is struggling with indecision or having difficulty taking action on a desire of their heart, it brings me great joy to coach them to see what needs to be done and figure out how to step out in faith and do it.

Recently, I met a lifelong friend for coffee to catch up and check in on each other's lives. After a while of what I like to call chick-chat, it was time to do what I enjoy doing most: ask questions.

I asked my friend how she was really doing. I asked about her dating life, her work life, her spiritual life, and her emotional well being. I asked her if she felt she was doing everything she could to maximize the life she had and if she was enjoying the benefits of a satisfied soul.

She said no.

When I prodded a bit, I learned that the main source of her struggle was that she hadn't been pursuing a dream of hers. She was clear on the goal, but overwhelmed when it came to taking action. All of the options prevented her from figuring out what she should do to get started. Inundated by more choices than she knew what to do with, she had done nothing.

So I asked her a few questions to help her move from desire to decision.

What was one thing she could do today to get the ball rolling? Was there a phone call she could make or a website she could review? Did she need to set up a meeting, make more time in her schedule, or remove a commitment to create room for a new one?

> **Some decision is better than no decision even if the decision you can make today is small.**

Some decision is better than no decision even if the decision you can make today is small. And don't despise the small things. Doing something that might seem insignificant is still doing something. Don't undermine your efforts by ignoring the one small thing you can do to move from thought to action. Small movements still contribute to momentum.

At nineteen, the thought of staying in college while raising a baby frightened the daylights out of me. I had no idea how all the jumbled puzzle pieces of my life could settle into a picture that made any sense. It was too much to figure out, and I honestly didn't feel capable of solving the whole puzzle in one sitting.

But there was something I could do.

There is always something you can do.

I picked up the phone and called an admissions counselor who had welcomed me into the school the previous semester. And I made an appointment to see him.

That was it.

Sure, I later investigated my options for housing and childcare. Sure, I had to eventually work at getting more scholarships, finding a job, and figuring out transportation. But my journey to finishing my degree started with my decision to make a phone call.

I'm not suggesting the decision you need to make will be easy or quick. I'm just telling you that your decision to move toward your girl isn't activated until you actually do something to set that decision in motion.

The move you need to make may seem hard, but you can pack one box.

The cost of college for your kids may seem daunting, but you can set aside a small amount of what you do have every month.

A habit of praying fervently may seem unattainable, but you can pray one prayer right now.

You may not know what job you are qualified to apply for, but you can scan the classifieds to see what's out there.

The relationship you need to end may threaten to rip your heart out, but you can write down the words you need to say and practice speaking them out loud.

I'm convinced that the enemy of good decision making is the inability or unwillingness to nail desires down to a next step. Desires become decisions when they are connected to an action.

Don't get stuck at the point of desire simply because you can't decide what to do. You could spend way too long wishing for change when the only thing standing between you and that change is your willingness to do something—anything—that kickstarts your journey.

> Desires become decisions when they are connected to an action.

Don't get stuck talking about change either. If you're not careful, you just might talk yourself out of the very thing God is trying to talk you into.

Yes, I know the struggle. But I've also learned the solution. The fastest way to escape analysis paralysis is to keep the main thing the main thing. You have to operate in light of where you hope to end up.

When Jessica McClure fell down that well, of course her mother wanted her out, but nothing happened until somebody decided to kick-start the rescue effort by calling for help. And you know why they made that call? Because they understood the main thing: getting the girl out.

> If you're not careful, you just might talk yourself out of the very thing God is trying to talk you into.

So how do you keep the main thing the main thing?

I'm glad you asked.

Habakkuk 2:2 says, "Write a vision, and make it plain so that a runner can read it" (CEB).

Based on this biblical principle, let me give you three steps to making a decision with your desired destination clearly in mind.

Step 1: Write It Down

Lee Iacocca once said, "The discipline of writing something down is the first step toward making it happen."[14] It's a proven fact that writing things down makes them more likely to happen. Writing things down is critical and important. No business could run without things being written down. Since your life is more important than any business, treat it that way by writing down the ways in which you want to grow, change, and become the person God wants you to be.

When God gave a vision to Habakkuk, He also told him to write it down. God knows that we are quick to be inspired, but often times slow to take action. When God gave the Ten Commandments to Moses, he had Moses write them down. In Revelation, when John experienced a vision of heaven, he was told by God to write down the things he saw.

God knows we are notorious for getting distracted and forgetting to live continuously with the end in mind.

When you write down the desires of your heart and the destination you hope to reach, you clarify your thoughts and reinforce your intentions for tomorrow based on aspirations you hold today.

Step 2: Remember It

Don't forget to keep your vision in plain sight. If you write your desires down and stick them in the side pocket of your purse to make friends with forgotten pieces of gum, loose change, or old lipstick, those desires will not be front and center in your mind or heart.

Write them down and put them somewhere you will see them. In your car. At your desk. As a reminder on your phone. Lipstick or Expo marker on your bathroom mirror will work too.

We need to be reminded of our intentions. We need to see them. We need a vision of the beautiful tomorrow that belongs to the girl in us, and we need to see this vision every day so we can remember to align our lives now with the girl we intend to be later.

So write down the dream that maybe you've forgotten or given up on. Write down that hope you harbor in your heart.

Post that Scripture with the command you need to follow, the encouragement you need to receive, or the message you need to remember.

And then look at it as often as possible so you never forget your destination.

Step 3: Rehearse It

Habakkuk was told to write the vision and make it plain so somebody else would know about the end game as well.

Something happens when you choose to share your destination with someone else. A friend of mine puts it this way: when you share your vision with someone else, you give it oxygen. And isn't that what we all need—a little room to breathe and believe that change is possible?

Now, pick something. Don't stress. Don't overanalyze. Don't wait for the perfect time.

Remember, the first key to living with focus is to make decisions that lead to actions—even small ones—that align with your aspirations.

So act. Seal your decision by connecting it with an action.

And know that even if you're a bit behind the eight ball—either from an indecisive period in your life or a period void of decisions at all—it's never too late to make a choice that gets you on your way.

Eventually, I made it to my grandfather's house and enjoyed the time I spent with him. He was happy to know I was coming and willing to wait for me once he knew I was en route to his front door.

Eventually, you will make it too.

And I know that the girl you want to be will be happy to see you.

Reflections for the Rescue

REMEMBER

Sometimes the best decision you can make is simply to make a decision.

REFLECT

- How have you seen analysis paralysis active in your life? What has analysis paralysis prevented you from accomplishing?
- Where in your life do you need to make a decision?
- Why do you think that decision has been hard to make?

RESPOND

Challenge yourself to make some small decision today. Solidify that decision by writing it down, putting it in a place where you can see it, and then pick up the phone and share it with someone else for accountability.

Philippians 3:13; Habakkuk 2:2; Proverbs 3:4–6; Joshua 24:15; Deuteronomy 30:15; Psalm 119:10–16; Revelation 2:5.

FORTY AND FAT

Maintain Your Direction
by Paying Attention

Forty and fat.

That pretty much sums it up.

Apparently me and my girl had a few too many hot chocolates.

With extra whipped cream, thank you very much.

One day, I looked in the mirror and realized I didn't recognize the person staring back at me. She was hidden by pizza, sweet tea, and French fries. French fries from Wingstop dipped in ranch, to be specific. (I'm almost sure those fries have crack in 'em.)

I was in a battle with the #fatdemon, and apparently I was losing—badly.

I stood frozen with surprise, gazing at the reflection of someone familiar, yet someone who only resembled the woman I expected to see staring back at me. I looked deep into my eyes and I saw *her*—the girl inside. I stood there for a long while pondering how it came to be that I'd neglected her.

While I understood that I was loved and valued, that knowledge was not connecting with care for myself—my body or my soul. I could see the uncared-for, abandoned version of my girl, and I realized I'd unintentionally buried her.

I'd drifted right up the scale, one small food decision followed by another, until I'd drifted right into the body of somebody else—except the body in the mirror belonged to me. In the absence of attentive living and vigilant choices, I'd drifted along the path of least resistance, a path paved with Hershey's Chocolate Kisses, dark-chocolate-covered almonds, and Wingstop fries. (About those fries, did you know they put *sugar* on those things!? #crack.)

Without attention, the drift just happened, one choice at a time.

Now, don't get me wrong, I know how to get rid of unwanted pounds. But while I'm good at losing the weight, I'm terrible at keeping it off. Keeping it off requires me to focus and to keep up that focus. It requires me to dig deep and then keep on digging.

My problem is that as soon as I lose some weight, I want to celebrate by, you know, going out to dinner. Or better yet, grabbing a 440-calorie Panera Bread Chocolate Chipper cookie.

Over the years, I've had my fair share of bouncing up and down the scale, but this time I'd quit trying. I'd given up. And my weight had ballooned.

Without treasuring the gift of the life that God gave to me, and without doing what was in my power to take care of myself, I looked up years down the road and realized that my health was way off course.

And the health of my soul was off course too.

The good news is that having battled the bulge for much of my adult life, I knew the antidote for mindlessly putting on the pounds. It just so happens to be the same antidote for unintentionally pulling the plug on your potential.

Pay attention.

It's that simple.

The Problem with Paying Attention

So if staying on track simply requires paying attention, why is staying on track so hard?

Let me explain by going back to the scale. Now, my goal here is not to make anyone feel bad about their extra pounds or imply that something is wrong with them if they're overweight. By all means, strive for good health and don't stress about being a perfect size six.

Food is good. It is what it is.

But mindless eating and aimless living both lead us to unintended destinations—extra weight we see on the scale or extra weight we feel in our souls.

Nobody plans on losing touch with the girl inside or feeling lost in her life, but without diligent effort, that's simply what happens over time.

The problem with paying attention is that it requires work. It doesn't just happen. Deliberate action is a prerequisite.

At any time, I have a closet full of clothes that span at least three sizes. Because, you know, I have to be flexible in this life. The truth is many times it's not until I go to put on an outfit I haven't worn in a while that I realize it doesn't fit.

> Mindless eating and aimless living both lead us to unintended destinations—extra weight we see on the scale or extra weight we feel in our souls.

For most of us, the scale simply tells the story of all the decisions we haven't really thought that much about.

No one goes to bed skinny and wakes up fat.[15] Most of us gain weight so slowly that we don't notice it happening. One day our pants don't fit, our bras are too small, and we look in the mirror and realize that our face is rounder than it used to be. And you don't even have to be a glutton for this to happen. Did you know that if you simply chew a stick of Doublemint gum every day for a year, at the end of the year you will be a pound heavier? (I know. I've ruined it for you. Now you'll never be able to look at a stick of gum the same way. So sad. Too bad.)

That's the thing. If you don't practice attentive living, your life will quickly morph into something you might not recognize or desire.

After losing a bunch of weight and keeping it off, singer and actor Jennifer Hudson said, "Permanent weight loss doesn't come with an on and off switch."[16]

I would agree, and I might add that permanent changes in life don't either.

If I plan on keeping off the weight I lose, maintaining the peace I find, or holding on to a deep-seated joy and love for the life I have, I need to consistently and regularly assess whether I'm staying on track and then do whatever it takes to get back on track if I've fallen off.

I shouldn't weigh in on the scale every five years, cross my fingers, and pray that nothing has changed. I shouldn't put on that certain pair of jeans just once a year and hope they'll still fit. And I can't look deeply into my own eyes every blue moon and expect to be doing a good job of cultivating the life and soul of the girl inside.

Right this very second, I have a wearable fitness device clipped on my bra between the two towers. That's right. Right in front of my sternum.

A few times a day, that little thing buzzes.

It takes all I have to remember I can't just reach down my shirt in front of random people to grope around and shut the doggone thing off.

I have set my device to buzz at certain times of the day to help me pay attention. It buzzes when I haven't moved in a while to remind me to get going. It buzzes around lunchtime to remind me to eat, since I have a terrible habit of skipping lunch when I'm busy with kids or hard at work in my office. It even buzzes with congratulations when I've reached my step goal for the day and flashes me a quick message of encouragement: "Way to go, Chrystal!"

Paying attention is important.

There is just one problem, though.

Paying attention takes effort.

Self-evaluation takes time and careful scrutiny.

The Practice of Paying Attention

Most of us don't practice paying attention to our lives. But paying attention should be a habit—a consistent and regular practice that keeps you aware and in touch with your life. It's different from looking at your life and making an initial assessment or a correction. Paying attention to your life is the habit that helps you to stick with the initial correction you made and to stay on track.

Proverbs 4:23 says, "Watch over your heart with all diligence, for from it flow the springs of life" (NASB).

> Paying attention should be a habit—a consistent and regular practice that keeps you aware and in touch with your life.

To nurture the person you want to be, you have to pay attention to—or "watch over"—your heart and your life. You have to fight to take notice of your soul and to guard the place from which you live. And this job must be done with diligence, which can be defined as continuous effort, conscientiousness, and hard work.

Did you get it? Digging deep and continuing to dig deep requires your effort.

This journey to your girl is going to require your participation.

A life lived with focus requires you to look and to keep looking.

This idea of continued effort is easy to understand when you look at the ways we already keep tabs on different areas of our life.

When you own a car, you need to change the oil, rotate the tires, and service the brakes. It requires maintenance. Every now and again you have to look—or have someone else look—at your car to see how well it's working.

If you create a budget to help you better manage your spending, the plan will only help you if every now and again you take a look at it. Without regular review, a plan for your spending won't help you.

I heard someone say that all relationships tend toward divorce. Whether it's a relationship with a spouse, a sister, or an assistant, without regular check-ins, relational assessment, and time spent examining the relational connection, people simply grow apart.

Most of us are aware that over time, things change and drift off course if we don't stay on top of moving in a certain direction. That's why we go to the doctor for checkups, deep clean our home, and dig up weeds in our yard. (Well, *some* of us deep clean our home and dig up weeds in our yard.)

To live with focus, we need to be willing to do the work of paying attention to our souls with the same diligence we pay attention to other areas of our lives.

Tips for Paying Attention

Allow me to share with you three simple ways to pay attention to your life.

First, take time to review. Remember when I told you in the previous chapter to write down the decisions you make? Well, something fantastic happens when you write them down. You get to see your progress! But only if you regularly review your written intentions.

Last year, I noticed I wasn't doing a good job of telling the people in my life that I love them. I felt it, many times I showed it, but I wasn't saying it. But because I think it's important to say those words every now and again, I decided to make my I-love-yous an area of focus for the next ninety days.

So I wrote the words "Say I Love You" in a little notebook I carry around with me, and as I spoke those words, I wrote down who I said them to. Seeing that written reminder helped me pay attention, and paying attention helped me to make a change that mattered to me.

After a while, I experienced great joy in seeing how far I'd come in being the person I wanted to be—someone who tells others how much they are loved.

Write down your decisions and, every now and then, review your progress. You will get so much joy from watching the unnecessary weight in your life fall off little by little over time.

Second, make time to retreat. Leave margin in your life for reflection. There simply ought to be time in your schedule to be still, to be quiet, and to be alone. If you always drive your car with your music blasting, you might miss sounds coming from your engine that can tell you something under the hood isn't right. Look at your schedule and pencil in non-negotiable time for you to hear yourself think, feel the rhythm of your soul, and see your life from an objective angle. Don't be legalistic about it. Just be intentional about looking at your life.

Regularly review your written intentions.

And as you contemplate your plan for pulling away, don't forget to prioritize prayer. Jesus himself had thirty-three years to be born, teach, train the disciples, and then die to save the world, yet He unapologetically withdrew from people to pray. If Jesus needed to break away to pray, then surely we do too.

Third, go to sleep! Get enough rest so that you have the clarity and capacity to be fully present in your life. Rest is the foundation on which you build everything else. And remember, even God rested on the seventh day.

If you wake up one day and realize you've drifted, that certain decisions have led you astray, or that something terribly hard in your life has thrown things out of whack, begin moving as best as you can in the desired direction, and pay attention to your progress.

If looking at the scale can help you maintain your weight, regular examination of the state of your soul can help you maintain your life.

I've never met a person who has lost weight and kept it off without an ongoing consciousness of what they put in their mouth. People who have long-term success with their weight practice the art of paying attention. So do people who have long-term success with their physical, emotional, and spiritual lives.

Leave margin in your life for reflection.

They have learned to live an attentive life.

Yes, paying attention takes effort, but you *can* develop the habit. And as you do, you will also start plugging in to your potential and realizing that you can recognize the girl in you.

Reflections for the Rescue

REMEMBER

Practice the art of paying attention.

REFLECT

- In what area of your life do you tend to drift off course?
- How do you know when you are drifting?
- How can paying attention to your life help you focus and stay on track?

RESPOND

What tip for paying attention resonates most with you? How will you utilize that tip in your day-to-day life? Think about your answer. Then write it down.

———————————

Ephesians 6:18; 1 Corinthians 16:13; Proverbs 4:23;
Psalm 32:8; Jeremiah 29:13; Psalm 19:14; 1 Peter 5:8–9.

———————————

CHAPTER

19

PEOPLE, PLACES, AND THINGS

Use Discernment

When you turn forty, you realize you're somewhere around the halfway mark on the march toward death, and you decide you ought turn up the volume on your life. If you haven't done it and still want to do it, you totally should do it. And do it as soon as possible.

My it? Running a marathon. So forty and still a little fluffy, I decided to try my hand at one. I didn't run it to celebrate my fortieth year, 'cuz it took me two years to admit I'd actually lived for four decades. Once I got a grip on reality, though, I made the decision and activated that decision by signing up and paying for the Dallas Marathon. (I'm still in disbelief at how much these races charge *me* to run for hours on end.)

When I signed up for the race, I had more than six months to prepare, so I found a plan that outlined checkpoints and gave me mini goals for my training.

The first goal was to run a 5K—3.1 miles of running nonstop. So I started moving in the direction of my goal by putting on my tennis shoes to run—well, at first mostly walk.

When I started out, I would run for a minute and then walk for a minute. The ratio of running to walking slowly shifted in favor of running, and before I knew it, I could go the 5K distance without stopping.

But training for a 5K is not equivalent to training for a marathon.

First of all, you can prepare for a 5K on a treadmill if you have to. When I started training, I preferred the treadmill in a temperature-controlled gym, thank you very much. (I live in Texas. A/C is important.) The treadmill also allowed me to watch the number of calories I burned add up. And if I needed a break, I could just stand on the side of the treadmill while the belt kept spinning and racking up the mileage. (Come on. I know I'm not the only one who's done that.)

But when it came time to train for the marathon, it's not as fun to run on a treadmill for hours on end. The scenery gets boring. And the treadmill doesn't prepare you for the changing conditions you'll face when you run 26.2 miles outside.

My new focus demanded my willingness to align my environment with my ambition. To be prepared for the marathon, I needed to train in the right conditions—outside, on the road, in the elements.

I also needed to start running with other people.

Normally I don't like working out with others. Who wants somebody else hearing you breathing hard? I also don't like to know *for sure* that I run like a turtle trudging through peanut butter. But when it was time to train for the marathon, I swallowed my pride and ran with others. I needed to be surrounded by people who had either done what I was trying to do or who were trying, like me, to achieve a new goal for the first time.

My preparation didn't stop there. All of a sudden I needed things to support me on my journey. I realized my shoes were terribly wrong for long-distance running. Who knew you could buy shoes based on the way your foot strikes the pavement? I also didn't know anything about energy drinks outside of Gatorade, or that there was such a thing as Gu—peanut-buttery stuff that gives you energy for running another couple of hours. I searched websites and flipped through running magazines for any tip

I could find. I didn't just change my environment and surround myself with people based on my new passion; I looked at anything that could help me cross that finish line.

Preparing for that marathon required me to exercise discernment in selecting people, places, and things that would keep me on track for reaching my goal.

Staying ready for your life will require the same.

People

You need to surround yourself with people who get where you're trying to go—people who can support you, join you, or give you some direction. If there are people in your life who don't do any of the above, it's your job to decide the amount of influence they have in your life—or whether they should be in your life at all.

Yes. It's that serious.

The people we allow in our lives can build us up, encourage us to be faithful, and help us follow through on the decisions we've made and the directions we've chosen, especially when we don't feel like sticking with the training plan.

If you're serious about doing the work of moving forward, you need to have people in your life who are serious about seeing you move forward too.

Three kinds of people can help you do just that—a pacer, a partner, and a promoter.

> If you're serious about doing the work of moving forward, you need to have people in your life who are serious about seeing you move forward too.

Pacers are people in long-distance races who have volunteered to run a certain pace for the duration of the race. The entire time they are running, they hold up a sign that displays their pace to let other runners know exactly how fast they're going. If you simply keep the pacer in view, they will keep you focused on the speed you need to go. A pacer is someone who runs in front of you, guiding you and helping you avoid unnecessary pitfalls because of their experience, maturity, or knowledge. They know how to run the race because they've done it before.

Partners are in the trenches with you, working to accomplish a goal you both share. When I trained for my marathon, I ran most of my long practice runs with a dear friend. While she'd run a marathon before, she preferred not to train alone. We held each other accountable and came alongside each other for mutual encouragement, accountability, and company.

Promoters encourage you and provide support. They believe in you, pray for you, and simply love to cheer you on. In some of the races I've run in, someone who knows me might show up for moral support at the finish line or somewhere along the course. But most of the time, the spectators I see along the way are strangers. Many of them line the course with signs. Some of the signs warm the heart, some are funny, and some of them provide a kick in the pants for me right at the moment I need it. While I have no idea who these people are, their presence and encouragement spur me on in my journey. Promoters are willing to campaign on your behalf. They believe you can do it, even if they've never done it themselves.

Sometimes your pacers, partners, or promoters are different people. Sometimes you'll find all three qualities in one person. But your job is to make sure you have at least one person in your life who can be one—or all three—of these to you.

Now, I know what some of you might be saying: "But I don't know anyone!"

Actually, you probably do know of someone. Jesus is the perfect pacer, partner, and promoter. He has shown us what it means to live a purpose-filled life (1 Peter 2:21–23). He is a friend who can be with us at all times (Luke 7:34; John 15:14). And He is constantly in our corner, showing His care and concern for us when He intercedes on our behalf (Heb. 7:25).

Start with Jesus. He's the only one who can be all of those perfectly.

We're also encouraged to have fellowship with others—someone we can touch, feel, and see. But here's the rub, my friend: you might have to do the work of searching that someone out.

When my husband and I decided to homeschool, I had no idea what learning at home could look like, so I cold-called a woman at my church who homeschooled and asked her if I could observe her teach in her home. Bold. I was just bold. I invited myself right into her living room for a whole day and positioned myself on her couch so I could watch and learn from her. This woman was my homeschooling pacer. Since that day, I've kept her in my view and reached out to her any time I needed advice or information.

Be willing to search out the person who has the information or experience you need. Ask good questions to get good answers. Get as close as you can to watch how they do it, and learn.

Maybe you need a partner. You could have a goal of writing or growing spiritually. Maybe you want to read or cook more often. Finding a partner can be as simple as asking someone you know if they'd be willing to regularly meet to write or pray. You might see if the other moms at your kids' school want to start a book club or swap recipes. When you need a partner, sometimes you have to be the partner you're looking for and invite your peers over for the Bible study, book club, or writers' group you really want to be a part of.

And if you need a promoter? The same applies to your need for encouragement. You must be humble enough to let people who are already present in your life know that you need someone promoting you, that you need their support and their prayers.

But what if you still can't think of your person?

Well, now, that leads us to the next area, an area in which you need discernment.

Places

I'm a slacker scrapbooker. While I like the finished product, I can never seem to work on my picture pages consistently when I'm alone. I'm not motivated. And since I haven't been to a scrapbook retreat in a while, my poor last child doesn't have a baby book (#momfail).

There's just something about sitting around a table scrapbooking with a bunch of other women that gets my creative juices flowing. If you're a student, you might feel this way about your studies. It's just easier to be productive at the library or a coffee shop where other people are being productive too.

When we choose environments—and people—that support our efforts, it becomes easier to do what we need to do. It is so important to set yourself in an environment conducive to your personal direction. It never ceases to amaze me how many people will complain about what they don't have, yet they don't position themselves to get it.

If you're in real need of community—with people who can surround you as you do the work of honoring the life God has given you—are you putting yourself in places where you will find the community you desire?

My oldest daughter and her husband are photographers. They started out doing graduation photos, family portraits, and some weddings here and there. Then they decided they wanted to increase their photography business by doing more weddings. So they started going to wedding expos. Lots of them. Just by virtue of being in that particular place, they got exposure to other people in the wedding industry and made connections to follow up on. Ultimately, their business exploded as a result of positioning themselves in the right place.

Sometimes it's not so much about making connections with people as it is about positioning yourself for success in some endeavor.

If you want to grow spiritually, you should attend church or a Bible study. When I was struggling with loneliness and having a regular quiet time, joining a weekly Bible study in my area met both my need for community and my need for consistency in the Word.

If you want to quit smoking cigarettes, you should get rid of the smokes in your house, stop holding on to loose change, and find something else to do during the time you would normally take a smoke break at work.

If you want to be more present during time with your family, you should designate a place for phones and other devices and have distraction-free spaces or times in your home.

If you want to lose weight, get the ice cream out of your house instead of hiding it on the back right corner of the third shelf in the freezer, like I sometimes do.

If you know that you need accountability to maintain your commitment to be celibate as a single person, get a roommate.

And if you want to develop a deeper relationship with God, create space in your life to be with Him. It might help to designate a place to meet—a certain chair, your car, your daily morning walk, or before your kids come barging into your bedroom in the morning. Keep a copy of His love letter to you in multiple places, like on your desk at work or in your purse, so you can read His words anytime, anywhere.

Align your environment with your ambitions.

Align your environment with your ambitions.

Your environment matters. The places and spaces where you do life can propel you forward into more of the life you want if you are willing to make the adjustments.

Things

Just last night, I saw a commercial for *American Ninja Warrior*, one of those shows that has contestants compete on obstacle courses. What got my attention was that the commercial focused on a competitor who was wearing a prosthetic. He was going to compete with one leg.

The statement he made during that thirty-second spot has resonated in my head: "I had cancer. The only way to save my life was to cut off my leg."

The commercial then cut away to scenes from the show where he is maneuvering the course with one fewer leg than everyone else.

But he was alive to do it.

He decided that if what was attached to him would stop him from living—even if it was a limb—he would have to let that thing go.

Every day, we're bombarded with things. Things to buy. Things to do. Things to watch. Things to read. Things to know. If we aren't careful, those things can suck the life right out of us. It's your job to make sure nothing gets in the way of living the way life was meant to be lived.

> **Sometimes we have to let go of what's killing us, even if it's killing us to let go.**

Sometimes we have to let go of what's killing us, even if it's killing us to let go.

Is the cost of the things you buy strangling your financial goals? Is the clutter in your home stealing your peace of mind? Is your addiction to social media robbing you of time to do something productive? Is the resentment you carry smothering the life out of the relationship you want to flourish? What things are infecting or affecting your precious and rare life?

This is what I know.

If you lack discernment, you will waste time.

When we're not picky about the people, places, and things we allow into our sphere of influence, we will never experience real living.

You don't have to waste any more time.

This is me.

Giving you permission.

Permission to set yourself up for success by searching out the right people and getting rid of the wrong people.

Permission to position yourself in the right place, making the adjustments in your space to make it easier for you to run.

Permission for you to keep the things that fill you and remind you both of who you are now and who you can be later.

Permission to be ruthless about getting rid of those things that steal from you and to be fearless about reaching for those things that will give you life.

You have permission to change and grow.

Increase the things in your life that push you toward the person you're trying to be and decrease the things that pull you away.

Exercise discernment in the people, places, and things you allow into your life. When it comes to your heart, your mind, your soul, and your body, be a ruthless gatekeeper who protects against things that will take from your life and a welcoming hostess for things that will give you life.

Years ago, I walked with one of my close friends during a season of extended grieving and pain. She was ready to be a mother. Twice she'd conceived, and twice she'd gotten to the five-and-a-half-month mark and lost her baby. Her body simply wouldn't hold her babies inside long enough for them to survive outside of her womb. She went through the physical pain of delivering each child, only to hold them in her arms and watch them slip away. I remember seeing her struggle through that dark time, distraught with the ache and longing to hold the children she'd birthed and the angst of wondering if she'd ever be able to do so.

> When it comes to your heart, your mind, your soul, and your body, be a ruthless gatekeeper.

But I didn't just get to watch her hurt. I've also had the gift of watching her heal. At some point, my friend knew that if she was going to move forward, she would need to set herself up to do so. She searched for other *people* who had experienced what she'd experienced. She reached out for help, allowing others to give her guidance, understanding, and a shoulder on which to cry.

I accompanied her to an event for mothers who'd lost their children pre- or post-natal. Mothers brought pictures of their babies, and boxes filled with newborn hats, hospital bracelets, and tiny footprints. In that *place*, mothers found understanding as they celebrated and wept together.

My friend went in search of *things*—resources on the web and books to educate herself, recommendations for doctors who might be able to assist her in pursuing a solution, and options should having biological children not be possible.

I've watched my friend journey through hurt, and I've witnessed her heal. Today, she is a mother to three living biological children and shares her testimony regularly with other women who are experiencing the same kind of pain she once felt.

She knows what it is to want to cry, scream, and shake her fists at God because of the oh-so-hard race she had been given to run. She knows what it is to feel stuck, as if one more day is not possible. But she also knows how important it is to surround herself with the people, places, and things that help her move forward.

Who do you want to be? What do you want to do? Where do you want to go?

Be deliberate about the choices you make regarding people, places, and things in and around your life.

Yes, you must be diligent to make a decision. Yes, you must pay attention so you maintain your direction. And yes, you must exercise discernment in selecting the people, places, and things that can help and support you on your way.

As of today, my marathon run happened two years ago. I ran right through the finish line and into a Cracker Barrel. I sat down and ate a big country breakfast and haven't gotten back to consistently running since.

But it's about that time, time for me to get back on track. The good news is I know what to do. Decision? Sign up for a race. Direction? Review my training schedule. Discernment? I know just who to call and just where to run.

And I'm sure there are some running shoes tucked away, hiding in the back of my closet.

Reflections for the Rescue

REMEMBER

Align your environment with your ambitions.

REFLECT

- Who do you have in your life who supports you, joins you, or gives you direction? Who are you supporting, joining, or giving direction to?
- How is your environment helping you focus? If it's not helping, what can you do to change that? What place will better position you to head toward your finish line?
- What things in your life create distraction? What things do you need in your life to help you be the person you're trying to be?

RESPOND

Take a piece of paper and make three columns on each side. On one side write "Good Discernment." List the people, places, and things that represent good discernment on your part. On the other side write "Poor Discernment." List the people, places, and things that illustrate your need to use more discernment in your life. Now pick something off the "Poor Discernment" side of the paper and decide what you can do to let that person, place, or thing go.

---

1 Corinthians 9:24; Hebrews 12:1;
Proverbs 27:17; Proverbs 17:17; Hebrews 10:24–25;
Romans 12:4–5; Romans 16:17.

A GIFT YOU GIVE YOURSELF

Exercise Discipline

The last time I wrote a book, both of my grandmothers were living. In that book, I expressed my gratitude for their long lives and their investment in my life.

This time as I write, I'm even more grateful, but I'm especially reflective because they both have passed away, leaving me the wonderful legacy of their love.

Their tenacity.

Their grit.

Their determination.

Their discipline.

My, oh my, those women were made of some tough stuff.

My dad's mom underwent a leg amputation the summer before she turned eighty years old. Postsurgical therapy is difficult for anyone, but when you're almost eighty? It's simply over the top.

I talked to my grandmother often after she'd been transferred to the rehab facility, and I listened to her describe how hard the therapy sessions were and how she was usually asked to do more than she thought she was capable of doing.

But she always did what they asked.

She wanted her life back.

Weeks later, after my grandmother was allowed to go home, I traveled across the country to visit her. And I got to see, with my own eyes, how hard her recovery was.

Every move made her wince.

Getting in the wheelchair. Dressing the wound. Getting into bed. Dealing with phantom pain.

But one thing made an impression on me more than anything else I witnessed.

During my stay, my grandmother had been fitted for a prosthetic. Her hope—and the hope of her doctors—was that she would be able to walk again. The only thing was she had to practice walking with the prosthetic leg.

The same woman who had just gone through a traumatic medical procedure had to put the very place where she'd experienced hurt into action if she wanted to move forward.

And she didn't want to.

She told me so.

But every day, twice a day, she put that prosthetic on the tip of her shortened limb, stood up with the help of a walker, and slowly but surely made her way to the front door. Once she got there, she made a tight U-turn in the hallway and then made her way back to her wheelchair to remove the prosthetic and breathe a huge sigh of relief.

My beloved grandmother did what she didn't want to do—doing what even pained her—because she knew that getting where she wanted to go required her disciplined participation in the process.

That's what discipline is. It's doing something because you've decided to do it whether you feel like it or not.

One of my favorite movies of all time is *The Great Debaters*. Denzel Washington is in it. Need I say more? He stars along with other great actors in a movie set in the 1930s in the middle of the Jim Crow South. The film is based on the true story of Melvin Tolson, a professor at Wiley College in Texas. Mr. Tolson formed the school's first debate team, which enjoyed great success competing against the country's top schools and eventually against Harvard in a national championship.

At one point in the movie, one of the debaters expresses his frustration to his father about the amount of work required to compete on the debate team. He laments the large investment of time, the difficulty of the preparation, and the pressure from Mr. Tolson.

The father, an educator himself, looks his son in the eye and delivers what, to me, is *the* line of the movie: "Son, we do what we have to do so we can do what we want to do."[17]

Bam.

Drop the mic.

Really, the movie could have ended right then.

But it didn't.

The film continued to illustrate what happened when the young students chose to embody the wisdom of those words and exercise discipline—doing what they didn't feel like doing much of the time. And it also illustrated so beautifully what it looked like for those kids to know victory.

Most of us can exercise some form of self-discipline when we need to.

We go to work.

We pay our bills.

We feed our kids.

We obey the law—sometimes. (Speed limits can be a problem for me.) We don't say the first thing that comes to mind—most of the time.

The problem is our lives are not always filled with things we need to do. Much of the victory we want to see in our lives is based on decisions we see as optional.

You can stay healthy for decades without bothering to exercise discipline, but after a while your body will let you know your lack of discipline mattered.

You can talk about your dreams and goals profusely, but after a while your lack of discipline will hand you disappointment and regret.

You can have every intention of developing deep connections with your family members and friends, but if you never discipline yourself to use your time wisely, those relationships will never blossom the way you hope.

Discipline is more than motivation. Discipline pushes past the desire to quit when motivation runs out.

Don't ask me how I know.

When I was dating in high school, I knew that healthy boundaries were important, but I didn't feel like setting them.

> Discipline is more than motivation. Discipline pushes past the desire to quit when motivation runs out.

When I struggled with perpetual tardiness in my twenties, I knew being late might get me fired, but when the alarm went off, I didn't feel like getting up.

When I desire deep fellowship with God, I know meeting with Him daily is the key to staying connected, but there are times when I feel like spending a few more minutes on social media more than I feel like carving out time with Him.

Motivation fluctuates or runs out because it's based on how we feel, and our feelings change constantly.

Discipline is the habit of acting in the moment based on a decision you made in advance, regardless of your feelings. It's the action that bridges the gap between your dreams and your reality.

> Discipline binds you by your will—not your emotions.

Discipline is the sinew that connects your decision, your direction, and the discernment you must use each and every day. It binds you by your will—not your emotions or the circumstances of any given day.

And most important, discipline is what gets you going again when you've screwed up, dropped the ball, or gotten off course. It compels you to move forward over and over again.

Why did I decide to run a marathon? I don't know.

To this day, I think it's one of the dumbest things I've ever done. Second to biking at screaming speeds down that long Sausalito, California, hill.

I think I signed up for the marathon because I'd had one brief moment of glory after a successful three-or four-mile run and thought I was marathon material. It's funny the games your brain will play in a few seconds of endorphin-inspired motivation. For a few moments, I thought I was an athlete, and I decided I was capable of running 26.2 if I put my mind to it.

A few months later, when I found myself dreading each long Saturday run, I kept working at my goal. Why? Because I was invested. Because I'd told friends, family, and basically everybody via social media that I was going to do it. Because I had committed. I wanted that medal.

But looking back, I realize there was more to it.

Little by little, with each Saturday run, I was exercising discipline—showing up, doing the work, regardless of how I felt. Sometimes the thread of your commitment is all that keeps you connected to your goal.

As the runs got longer and harder, as much as I wanted to skip runs here and there, I did them anyway. I had developed the habit of doing what I didn't feel like doing, and that habit helped me stick with my decision.

That same habit of discipline didn't just help me prepare for my race; it helped me to finish it.

A few months later—December of 2014, to be exact—my finish looked nothing like I'd envisioned. It was quite depressing. It rained. I clocked my slowest pace ever. My rocking marathon playlist was of no use when my phone got wet and died with ten miles still to go. When I finally crossed the finish line, very few people were still there. Most of the supporters had cheered on their friends and family who had finished long before me and had already gone home. The volunteers who so energetically had lined the course and post-finish had helped with medals, snacks, and photo-ops had thinned out considerably, as most had met their time commitments and gone home.

I run like a turtle in molasses, remember?

Or is it peanut butter?

Maybe it was both mixed together, because I felt like I was going nowhere fast.

Can I be honest? Initially, it was a bit deflating. My expectations of what the finish would look like were not met—at all. But that's not the whole story.

I remember the slow realization of something important. I had crossed the finish line. I'd had a goal. And I'd finished. Sweaty, stinky, tired, and sore, I'd accomplished what I'd set out to do.

What is your finish line? Is it financial freedom, professional fulfillment, physical health, a happy marriage, or spiritual growth and maturity?

Truth be told, we have multiple courses to complete in various seasons of our lives. We want to run well in our work and in our relationships, making time for rest, recreation, and reflection along the way. We want to run well with our dreams and with the desires of our hearts, leaving nothing on the table when it's our time to leave this earth, knowing we gave all we had to give.

You have to think enough of yourself to believe that when God gave you legs, He meant for you to use them. You've got to fight laziness, tell yourself no when necessary, and get moving when you're tempted to stand still. But finishing well requires the practice of discipline—building habits that keep you showing up and doing the work regardless of how you feel.

So decide to do something. Start small—one step at a time—and gradually increase your distance as you increase your endurance.

Less than one-tenth of one percent of the world's population has finished a marathon. That's because it's hard. It takes work, dedication, and discipline. Only a small percentage of people in this world have been willing to work toward that high level of their physical potential.

Do you want to be the full expression of who God designed you to be? Do you want to reach your full potential?

Then you can't sit around and hope that by some measure or magic, the life you want will come to you. You have to exercise the discipline it takes to get up and run.

You may run fast. You may run slow. You may scream like a banshee during some miles or sob uncontrollably during others. On some legs of the journey, you may have cheerleaders, and on others you may find yourself alone. You will have parts with pain, parts with joy, and parts where you're just getting through. But if you keep at it, if you cross the finish lines that lie before you in the various areas of your life, you will win.

How do you develop discipline? You practice. You show up. You work at it. You operate with priorities. You put first things first. And then you do it again and again.

Discipline requires doing what you have to do so you can do what you want to do.

Want to be healthy enough to enjoy retirement? You have to take care of your body.

Want to enjoy financial stability? You have to stop spending money you don't have to buy things you don't need.

Want to be ready for the man of your dreams? You have to stop wasting time and sharing your soul with the men who aren't.

> Discipline requires doing what you have to do so you can do what you want to do.

Want to have a life filled with passion and purpose? You have to spend time following the instructions He's already provided.

Want to know God's will for your life? You have to take the small opportunities you have right now to use the gifts He has given you. Be faithful in the little things.

Luke 16:10 says, "If you are faithful in little things, you will be faithful in large ones. But if you are dishonest in little things, you won't be honest with greater responsibilities" (NLT).

When I realize that I need to work on building discipline in spending time with the Lord, the first task at hand is to wake up early, before my kids start demanding breakfast. I look at my bedtime routine to make sure I'm setting myself up for success to get up when that alarm goes off. I also build in rewards that motivate me in other ways. I love hot tea, so when I wake up I make my way to the kitchen, heat up the water, and grab a peppermint tea bag. Another thing that fills me up is coffeehouse music, so I find some on Spotify and pipe it through the speakers.

Now I'm ready. With peppermint tea in hand and coffeehouse music in the background, I crack open my Bible to read and be nourished in the Word.

Discipline isn't easy, but it's necessary. It takes reprogramming your habits and your thoughts, as well as mastering your emotions. Yet it's essential. The discipline with which you live your life will be the foundation on which you live a life you love. Discipline isn't easy, but it's worth it.

Do what you have to do now, so you can do what you want to do later.

When I left my grandmother's house, I left her still practicing walking back and forth to the door.

Not too long after that visit, she sent me a text. (Yes, my grandmother texted me on a regular basis, sent me emails, and occasionally stalked me on Facebook.) It was my precious grandmother sending me a photo of herself at the bottom of her front porch steps, holding on to her walker and standing on two legs—one real and one not so much.

There were no cheerleaders. There was no medal. There was no fanfare. The race had been hard, and her progress may have been slow.

> The discipline with which you live your life will be the foundation on which you live a life you love.

But she'd won.

It had only been a few months before that I'd visited her and seen her discipline in action. That visit holds the last memories I have of physically being in her presence.

But those memories have made an indelible impression on me.

And when I ran my marathon, I thought of her.

I thought of how hard she worked simply to walk down her front steps. I thought of the pain she endured and the tears she cried. And I thought that, if she were alive on the day I decided to enter the race, she would have told me to run.

Even if I was tired.

Even when I felt indifferent.

Even if it rained.

I know she would tell me to exercise the discipline required to run my race well, because she knew the joy of the finish.

I hope my grandmother's discipline makes an indelible impression on you.

When you choose to exercise discipline and do what you know you should based on decisions you've made—especially in the moments when you feel the least like doing them—you're giving a gift to yourself.

The gift of a life well lived.

The gift of less regret.

The gift of deep satisfaction.

All a gift to the girl in you.

Reflections for the Rescue

REMEMBER

The discipline with which you live your life is the foundation on which you live a life that you love.

REFLECT

- Have you ever had a goal that you gave up on because of how you felt?
- Where in your life do you have discipline? Where do you lack discipline?
- If discipline is the vehicle through which you accomplish your goals, habits are the tracks on which discipline runs. What habits in your life need to be broken? What habits do you need to build?

RESPOND

Discipline is based on actions you do whether or not you feel like doing them. Think of one small task that you have been avoiding. Get up and do it. Practice makes perfect. Discipline is a muscle that you can build.

---

1 Timothy 4:7; Romans 13:14; Daniel 1:8; Titus 2:12;
Hebrews 5:11–14; 1 Corinthians 9:25–27; Hebrews 12:11;
Proverbs 12:24; Proverbs 20:13; Proverbs 25:28.

FIVE TO SEVEN
YELLOW LINES

Just Keep Going

A few years ago, my sister and her husband bought their current home. It wasn't too far from where I lived at the time, but it was in an area of town that I wasn't familiar with.

One evening, as the sun was beginning to set, my sister called to invite me to see her new house. I hesitated. It was going to be dark soon, and I wasn't sure I felt like finding a new location at that time of day. The other reason I hesitated was because I was already comfy at home in my T-shirt and yoga pants. The bra had been pulled off and the fuzzy socks were in full effect.

For all intents and purposes, the day was over.

But my sister really wanted me to come, so I got up and got myself together (yes, I did put my bra back on) and headed out to her new digs.

The directions were straightforward.

Leave my house. Make a left. Drive a mile. Make another left. Drive eight miles. Make another left, then turn into her driveway.

Simple enough.

After making the second left turn, I found myself on a road with six lanes, a median, and plenty of street lights to illuminate the road. However, after just a few minutes, the landscape changed. The six-lane road became a four-lane road. I was grateful the median was still there.

The sun was just beginning its descent below the horizon, and I held out hope that I'd make it to my destination with a fully lit sky.

Not long after, the scenery changed yet again. The trees grew taller and thicker, blocking out the little light that was still available. Four lanes narrowed to two, and the median disappeared.

So did the street lights.

I found myself gripping the steering wheel a little tighter, squinting to narrow my focus on the road. Doubt crept into my head. Why am I on this unfamiliar road, going to an unfamiliar place, at an unsettling time of day? Maybe I should turn around and try this trip in the daytime when I can confidently navigate my way into new territory.

Isn't this how life feels sometimes?

When we head in a new direction, begin a new journey, or travel someplace unknown or uncharted, there's always a level of discomfort associated with the voyage.

The experience can be uncomfortable.

Unanticipated.

Unsettling.

I'd been convinced when I'd talked with my sister that the trip would be worth it, but now I wasn't so sure. I'd started down the long, curvy road, but the decision of staying on that road was up to me. As I contemplated turning around, I noticed something.

Yellow lines.

Slowly, as my eyes fought to focus in this new, dark place, I realized the path in front of me was marked with a consistent rhythm of stripes painted down the middle. The dashed yellow line was there guiding me, leading me, and directing me.

At this point, my bright lights were on, and I intently focused on the road in front of me. I had no idea where I was going, and I'd quickly developed a dependence on those yellow lines. The thing is I could only see about five to seven of those yellow lines at a time.

But five to seven yellow lines were all I needed to see.

As long as I kept my eyes on those yellow lines, I knew whether I was headed uphill or downhill, or whether a bend in the road was coming soon. As much as I would have preferred to see the full landscape in the light of day, the yellow lines told me all I needed to know.

As long as I kept my eyes on them.

The paths of our lives are also marked—marked with our gifts, abilities, interests, passions, and natures. They're marked by our experiences, both positive and painful. And they're marked by our opportunities, relationships, and choices.

Our lives are full of yellow lines, even if we only see the few that lie right in front of us.

The beautiful singing voice God has given you is a yellow line.

Your passion for children's health and safety is a yellow line.

The challenge you wouldn't have chosen but overcame is a yellow line.

Your sense of humor is a yellow line.

An important part of journeying through this life is to focus on what you can see and to keep moving. Don't be distracted or disappointed by what you can't see or what you can't figure out, but be diligent in focusing on what's right in front of you and faithfully following through. All you may have to follow are five to seven yellow lines, but if you're willing to commit to the journey, that's all you need.

In the words of Dory the fish (whom I've come to know almost as well as I know Barney the dinosaur), "Just keep swimming."

This is the part of living that jacks most of us up. We make the connection. We experience the moment of motivation. We feel the joy of a soul set on fire. We decide to do something about the pain. We take one step, maybe even two.

We start.

But we don't keep going.

How do I know? Because I've done it a few times in my own life.

Motivated, inspired, or stimulated by some talk I heard, some book I read, some person I met, or some place I went, I started out strong. But then—when things got difficult or boring—I quit.

Stopped swimming.

When we find ourselves on a seemingly solitary journey, a path that appears to have no purpose, or a long road with less light than we'd like, we doubt our decision to begin in the first place. Or we simply don't exercise the discipline to stick with the program.

And this place, my friend, is where many of us abandon the adventure of truly living. Most of us don't like traveling in the dark. We prefer not to stay in places that make us feel uneasy. We don't want things to be hard.

So we doubt.

We hesitate.

We give up.

We decide not to embrace the process of the passage, the work of the rescue, the labor of loving God's image in us.

We slide off the cornerstone of real connection, right back into the familiar discomfort of yet another crisis, and we start over.

We pull into an unfamiliar driveway, turn around, and go home.

Again.

If you avoid productive discomfort, you'll only be distracted and delayed from arriving at your desired destination. If you sidestep the discomfort now, you might also sidestep the peace and joy you hope for later.

Can I just stop right here and tell you that I've stopped and started over more times in my life than I care to admit? Nobody wants to be uncomfortable, including me. There have been times that, while I felt drawn to the girl I could be, something about the journey required more of the right-now me than I wanted to give.

So I quit.

I stayed in the relationship way too long. I didn't want to be lonely.

I spent more money on right now rather than saving for later. I didn't want to wait.

I took care of everyone else, but I didn't do a good job of taking care of myself. I felt guilty for taking me time.

I started reading through the Bible but didn't finish. I slept in late or went to bed early.

I chose healthier foods and activities—for a hot second. I skipped the salad and went straight for the chocolate.

Sound familiar?

Maybe you've tried to get something good going in your life.

Maybe you started counseling but didn't continue. The meetings were inconvenient, or the counselor asked hard questions you didn't want to answer.

Maybe you started the degree but didn't complete it. You were tired of not having a social life or maybe sick of doing the work.

Maybe you joined the small group but didn't attend for long. You were overwhelmed with the commitment required to be in meaningful community.

Maybe you prayed about it but didn't keep praying about it. It was easier to settle for the worst than to hope for His best.

Can you think of a yellow line you might have seen but chose not to follow? A connection you've made but haven't remained committed to? A discomfort or difficulty that got in the way of you moving farther in your life and on your journey?

Do what you can with what you have to move in that direction.

Then keep moving.

The point is not only to make a connection but also to keep making that connection.

Never forget that every journey is a process. The key to your journey is to start and then keep going. Know that every journey takes time. The key to living fully is the willingness to go with whatever light you have, to trust the process and believe that whoever painted the yellow lines in and around you knew what they were doing.

My mother has always told me, "When you don't know what you are supposed to do next, just continue doing whatever God told you to do last."

> The key to your journey is to start and then keep going.

You're probably reading this book because something has called you to attention. Maybe it's a crisis of identity. Maybe you're panicking a bit because you've recently awakened to how far you've drifted. Maybe some decision has put you in an unanticipated situation. Maybe a collision of your own doing—or someone else's—has put you into a full-on tailspin.

Maybe life has simply not been kind to you.

Whatever the reason, the girl inside is still there, calling you, beckoning you to answer and then to keep answering.

Your decision to do what you can with what you have—and then to keep following those yellow lines—is how you will make real, lasting progress.

God has given you everything you need to live your life. But He will not live it for you. Living requires your participation.

Your road might not always feel good. Whatever motivation got you going on your journey will probably wane. The unfamiliar will feel uncomfortable, and the unknown will feel unsettling. You might be tempted to turn around and restart the journey.

Inspiration can start the engine, but what keeps you moving forward is the dedication to keep your hands on the wheel and your foot on the pedal.

The night I went to visit my sister, I felt uncertain and unsure in the dark.

But I stayed on the road.

I focused on those yellow lines all the way to my sister's driveway because the person who called me was worth the trip.

As you think about the journey God has you on today—and the energy it takes to keep following the yellow lines—remember that you are worth the trip. Rediscovering the girl inside is worth pressing through twists and turns and the discomfort of darkness when your destination isn't yet in sight.

> God has given you everything you need to live your life. But He will not live it for you.

Oh, and there's this other thing. That was the first of many trips I would make down that road over the next few years.

Not long after that first trip, I moved into a house next door to my sister. The trip I almost abandoned ended up being a trip I not only grew accustomed to but also learned to love. Those yellow lines became familiar, even comforting, because I knew that they were leading me home.

People ask me all the time how I've made it through difficult seasons. They wonder what secrets I have to share for surviving hurt, heartbreak, and heavy loads. They want me to tell them how I function on days when it's hard to go one more step or one more mile, or to hold fast to hope after yet another disappointment.

Here's what I've done. I've become familiar with the road. I've learned that the destination is sweet but the journey itself can be even sweeter. Staying on the road is worth it because you learn so much about your girl along the way.

The road is unfamiliar, the way is simple. Stay the course. Do the next thing. Keep doing the next thing.

A young widow, Ruth did the next thing, and then kept doing the next thing. Motivated by love for her mother-in-law, a heart to do the right thing, and a desire to know the God of the Israelites, she left her home, faced an unknown future, and took a chance on finding a new life while leaving her familiar life behind. She found a new love and a new purpose, and this pagan woman found herself right smack-dab in the lineage of Christ.

An orphan, Esther did the next thing, and then kept doing the next thing. Motivated by a love for her people, respect for wise counsel, and the recognition that her opportunity also came with responsibility, she risked a life of luxury and royalty for the survival of an entire race. Esther solidified her place in the palace and in history as a woman of power—soft, strong, shrewd, and graceful.

A prostitute, Rahab realized she had a chance to save herself from the life she'd created when one day she invited men into her home—not to service them but to serve their cause and their God. Motivated by a hope for more, a healthy fear of the Israelite God, and a will to survive impending disaster, she took the risk of a lifetime. Rahab teaches us that it's never too late, that we have never fallen too far, and that God's grace can reach anyone, anywhere, at any time. Rahab made the connection and then kept making the connection.

> It's never too late. We have never fallen too far. God's grace can reach anyone, anywhere, at any time.

Make the connection with your girl. Wake up. Know what you carry, and use it. Know what ignites your soul, and do it. Know why you feel pain, and deal with it. Do what you can now, and keep doing it.

Then trust in the one who created you and the one who watches over the road you travel, five to seven yellow lines at a time.

Reflections for the Rescue

REMEMBER

The key to your journey is to start, and then to keep going.

REFLECT

- What yellow lines are on the road of your life? How is your life marked with your gifts, abilities, interests, and nature?
- Have you ever tried to follow those lines? Did you stop? Why or why not?
- What have you started that you just needed to keep working to finish? Do you know enough to go? What's getting in the way?

RESPOND

- Sometimes we don't need new information, we just need to utilize the information we already have. What do you already know about your life that you just need to start acting on? Make the decision. Put a date on your next step in that direction. And do it.
- Talk to God about your desire to keep moving forward in the life He has given you. Commit to Him that you will keep moving down the road of your life starting with your next step.

Proverbs 3:6; Galatians 6:9; Hebrews 11:1;
2 Thessalonians 3:13; 2 Corinthians 5:9; Philippians 2:12–13;
Hebrews 10:36; Colossians 1:11; Romans 5:3–5.

PART 5

ENCOURAGE YOUR LIFE

Watch your mouth: The language we use creates the reality we experience.

—*Michael Hyatt*

It's never too late to design the life you love.

—*Lysa TerKeurst*

CHAPTER

22

BE YOUR OWN
BEST FRIEND

Coach Yourself

Michelle Carter is a world champion, an Olympic gold medalist, and an American record holder in women's shot put.

She is good at what she does and knows how to live with focus. Her professional career is based on decisions she made a long time ago, a direction she has remained committed to, discernment she uses every day, and discipline that keeps her at the top of her game.

Michelle makes winning look easy.

She walks out onto the field with rhythm and ease, and uses her body to throw an almost nine-pound ball many meters.

It's clear that Michelle knows what she is doing.

Michelle is a friend of mine, and when she was preparing for the Olympic Games in Rio—where she won the gold medal—I asked her what it has taken for her to keep her focus and continue to have a successful career.

Michelle's response? She has learned to coach herself.

Michelle has learned what it means to be her own best friend.

When she gets tired of doing all the things that have gotten her where

229

she is now, she encourages herself to keep doing them. Michelle also coaches herself when she's on the field getting ready to throw that metal ball. She walks herself mentally through the movements she's thoroughly practiced and talks herself, sometimes audibly, through her game.

"Okay, girl, you know how to do this."

"Stay relaxed."

"Be patient. Don't rush it. Give your legs time to generate the power you need to throw."

Michelle understands the importance of coaching herself by being her own encourager when necessary, even if that means talking out loud to herself on the field.

God has given us an opportunity to use all He has put in and around us to fully engage in this life. With every breath we take, we inhale another possibility, another moment to honor Him with attitudes and actions that bring Him glory, bless others, and honor the unique gift of the girl inside us.

If we are willing to focus on doing our part.

If focus is central—the hub in the wheel that moves your life forward—then your decisions, direction, discernment, and discipline are the spokes—your efforts to set things in motion. But what it takes to start making progress is not always enough to keep making progress. Like a wheel, the hub of your life also needs a rim. Your ability to coach yourself is that rim.

It is good to have people in your life who cheer you on or give you guidance, but you must be willing to encourage yourself so you can keep your momentum going.

While it's wise to have a mentor or guide, the only person who will be with you for all of your life, all of the time, is you! If you can befriend yourself and coach yourself, especially when the process of your progress is wearing you out, you will have the wherewithal to stick with it and stay in motion.

And like any coach anywhere, your encouragement will involve using words.

Use Your Words

Our words matter.

Proverbs 18:21 says that "the tongue has the power of life and death." You will believe what you tell yourself, so be careful what you say.

It is your job to get up every day and coach yourself, to tell yourself who you are, whose you are, and what you expect yourself to do.

Your commitment to moving forward requires you to encourage yourself, whether or not anyone else is encouraging you. Choose to regularly honor the girl inside of you with words of acceptance and affirmation based on her inherent God-given value.

> You will believe what you tell yourself, so be careful what you say.

I challenged you earlier in our journey together to tell yourself that you're okay, but now I want you to understand how important it is to do even more than that with your words. I want you to come up with words that affirm your value and say them to yourself on a regular basis, particularly when you are facing something hard.

Even David, the great warrior, faced times of great discouragement and difficulty. When he faced defeat at the hands of his enemies and rejection by those who claimed to be his friends, David "encouraged himself in the LORD his God" (1 Sam. 30:6 KJV).

David chose faith in the God who made him and belief in the purpose God had for his life, even when moving forward seemed hard and he felt like quitting. And he encouraged himself to keep going.

Speaking life to your heart and to your situation may mean speaking God's truth out loud as you look yourself in the eye. Speaking life simply

_____

Learn to be your own best friend.

_____

means speaking kindly to yourself and encouraging yourself just like you would a good friend. And it's worth learning to be your own best friend, even if it means talking to yourself out loud every now and again.

Speak kindly.

Speak with love.

And truth.

Wherever you see the need *for* change in your life, start speaking that change *into* your life. The power to do so lies in your own tongue.

Coach Your Life with Your Lips

Maybe you need to tell yourself that you're a good mother if you have teenagers who don't make you feel that way. Maybe you need to rehearse that you're a strong woman who chooses to live with purpose even while you sit in traffic yet another morning. Maybe you simply need to remind yourself each and every day that you are loved by God and then walk with confidence in your inherent value.

We can be tempted to rehearse what we see when we look in the mirror right now or repeat our feelings about our situation today. But if your tongue has the power to give life, you should coach your girl by speaking confidently to her about who she is, what is possible, and what she can become.

Maybe when you look in the mirror you don't like what you see. You might find yourself saying, "I'm fat," or, "I don't like my shape." You might lament the shape of your nose, the wrinkles in your skin, or the gnarly gray hairs that grow back faster than you can pluck 'em.

But if you choose to rehearse only what's wrong with you, you'll only be putting effort into tearing yourself down. While you should do what you can to change what positively affects your health, use your words to endorse that you are a unique, beautiful creation—crooked nose, wrinkly skin, gnarly gray hairs, and all.

Instead of saying, "I'm fat," you can say, "I am the best me I can be right now, and every day I have the power to do something to move in the direction of a healthier version of me."

Instead of saying, "I'm getting old," you can say, "I'm so blessed to have lived long enough to gain wisdom, maturity, and experience. If God could use me when I was twenty, I wonder how He's going to use me to make a difference in this world now!"

It's all in how you look at it, and it's all in how you choose to speak to the girl in you.

Overwhelmed? You might be, but don't rehearse that. Once you acknowledge your situation, don't live there. Speak life to yourself, reminding your girl she has the power to be both the keeper of her schedule and the keeper of her attitude about the things she cannot control. You could say, "I feel overwhelmed right now, but I can choose to remove something from my life that will open up more time in my schedule."

Stuck in a job you don't like? Don't rehearse that you hate your job. Rehearse the gifts, skills, or abilities you can cultivate now to prepare for the next opportunity that will come your way.

Silence the negative self-talk.

Tired of being alone? While you may feel lonely, don't talk about that state of mind and heart more than you talk about how you are a good friend, sister, or mentor. You have the power to initiate and create connection in your life every day!

Silence the negative self-talk. The girl in you needs to hear that you believe in her. Affirm who you are, whose you are, and what is possible.

Fight for *you*.

While Michelle Carter is an accomplished athlete and regularly coaches herself on the field, she doesn't stop there. Michelle is also a motivational speaker.

The opportunity to share encouragement with others has come by way of her success as an athlete, but speaking has not always been Michelle's most comfortable playing field.

Michelle has ADD and dyslexia. She struggles with words. She used to hesitate when asked to speak in front of others because she didn't want to mess up the words, sound stupid, or not be able to express herself clearly.

The same self-coaching Michelle uses on the field has served her well when in front of a mic.

"Okay, girl, you know how to do this."

"Stay relaxed."

"Be patient. Don't rush it. Give your mind time to generate the words you want to share."

Because speaking hasn't always been comfortable for her, Michelle has learned to draw on other sources of encouragement as well.

"You may be ADD and dyslexic, but that's how God made you."

"You are worthy of this opportunity."

"You have not been given a spirit of fear."

"You can do all things through Christ who strengthens you."

Whether Michelle is on the field or in the front of an auditorium, she coaches herself by letting her head lead her heart and her actions by using her words. She encourages herself, reinforcing the focused preparation and practice that have led her to this point. Michelle rehearses what she knows to be true about herself and what she knows to be true about her God, both in her mind and with her mouth.

Be willing to encourage yourself. Even if it means being the woman who talks to herself out loud every now and then, be a good friend to *you*. Rehearse what is true and good about you in light of what you know to be true about the God who created you.

Pursue progress in your life, and reinforce your efforts by coaching yourself along the way.

Reflections for the Rescue

REMEMBER

Silence the negative self-talk.

REFLECT

- When it comes to how you talk about yourself and your life, do you normally lean to the positive or the negative? Why do you think that is?
- If you were a good friend to you, what would you say about yourself? How would you encourage yourself?

RESPOND

- Think of three encouraging statements a good friend might say about you. Write those things down. Keep that list handy, and when you find yourself being more critical of yourself than you are supportive, use your mouth to coach yourself.
- Pick one of those statements and say it out loud, right now, to yourself.

Psalm 19:14; Psalm 141:3; Proverbs 4:24; Proverbs 13:3; Proverbs 18:21; Luke 6:45; Ephesians 4:29; James 3:4–5.

CHAPTER 23

THE MONSTER IN YOUR MIND

Coach Your Head

O ur family had just moved to the country, and I was gradually getting used to the remote location.

I could see nothing in front of my house except my driveway and the trees beyond. The rear view was no different. Large windows looked out onto a grassy area sprinkled with towering trees. As much as I loved the view, when we first moved into the long, one-story, ranch-style house, it took a while to get used to the quiet, the critters, and the peculiar noises this city girl wasn't familiar with.

One night, I stepped out of the shower and realized I hadn't yet retrieved my clothes from the dryer in the laundry room. The pajamas I needed were in that load. Since the house was quiet with everyone already tucked in bed, I wrapped myself in a towel and started the trek to the laundry room at the other end of the house.

Tiptoeing with damp feet down the hallway, I passed by the large windows at the back of the house. As I glanced through them into the darkness, a little unnerved that we hadn't yet covered them, I caught a glimpse of something that stopped me dead in my tracks.

I saw a man in the darkness looking back at me.

Immediately, my heart started pumping a flood of adrenaline through my body. There I stood, half-naked and dripping just a tad, frozen, unable to move a muscle as my brain worked overtime to figure out what to do.

I wasn't sure whether to run forward or backward. I had no idea if he was there to prowl or if he was just as surprised to see me as I was to see him. I didn't know if he would turn away in embarrassment or charge toward me in aggression.

I stood there for what felt like an eternity, trying to gather my druthers and decide what to do.

He stood there too, lurking in the shadows.

Eventually, I figured I needed to get myself together and get control of the what-ifs that plagued my thoughts. The wrestling with racing ideas wouldn't change my situation any more than wrangling them would. So I coached myself into sliding one slippery foot slowly in front of me to see what response it produced from the monster man outside my window.

He didn't move.

So I moved another foot forward, ever so carefully.

He still didn't move.

As I began to take the third step, I peered more intently into the darkness at the man who'd threatened my security only to realize it wasn't a man at all. It was only the moon's light outlining some low-hanging branches in the trees.

I felt like an idiot. I'd lost my ability to breathe, take action, and move forward because of a figment of my imagination. I could have slipped and broken my neck over something that didn't even really exist. I'd been so busy staring into the darkness that I'd lost sight of the light.

While I may not be able to keep you from losing your marbles as you creep down the hallway in the middle of the night, I hope I can impress upon you the importance of cultivating a healthy thought life. You will have difficult moments when the monster in your mind may seem very real indeed, but if you can learn how to coach yourself to think right thoughts, you can keep moving forward.

Just recently, finding myself plagued by thoughts that threatened to keep me from making progress, I've been reminded of the importance of coaching myself by coaching my head.

When I started writing this book, my excitement about both the topic and the opportunity to share it propelled me forward. I had more words than I knew what to do with, as well as tons of energy to put those words down on paper. Starting the journey was not the problem.

It was after I'd gained a little momentum that I found myself staring into the dark unknown, confronted by thoughts that stopped me dead in my tracks.

The monster in my mind had made an appearance.

I struggled with doubt, wondering if I could really help anyone, craft words worth reading, and write a book anyone would even want to finish. I felt naked and vulnerable as I ruminated on the darkness—the negativity in my mind.

While the monster in your mind might not take your physical life, incorrect thinking *can* kill. It can kill your hope, it can kill your joy, and it can kill your motivation to push past momentary problems or pressure toward the purposes God has placed in you.

Wrong thinking can steal the life that the girl in you would love to live. So it's urgent that you learn to coach yourself by controlling thoughts that make their home in your head.

When you focus on thoughts that are inaccurate or fragments of the truth, those thoughts can keep you frozen in fear. If you stare only into the darkness, you'll quickly lose sight of the light. Just like my wrong thinking about the man in the dark kept me from taking steps down the hallway, wrong thinking can inhibit you from moving forward in your life.

Every day after I wake up and make my way to my bathroom, I am faced with something that gently coaxes me out of my self-deprecating corner and inspires me to keep moving.

Early on in my book-writing adventure, I came home one day to find sticky notes posted all around my bathroom mirror. Those sticky notes stare at me each day and tell me that

- I am a good writer.
- I am good enough.
- I am the only person who can write like me.
- My opinions and experiences matter.
- I have ideas and creativity that are worth sharing with the world.

But I didn't put those sticky notes there. My sister did.

When I look in the mirror to wipe the matter from my eyes, I can't help but see messages designed to remind me of who I am and what I'm capable of accomplishing. Over and over, those words around my mirror have coached me, encouraging me to slide out from my motionless mentality, move my feet, and keep going.

Thoughts matter.

And learning to think right thoughts is one of the ways you coach yourself.

My sister wanted to help me. She understood how important it was for me to fight the destructive thoughts that threatened to uproot what God has planted in me.

⌒

Regardless of what is happening in your life, your thinking can either paralyze you or propel you. Remember, Proverbs 23:7 says, "For as he thinks in his heart, so is he" (AMP).

Your thoughts permeate your heart and soul and then overflow into what you do. How and what you think affects how you live.

Get your thoughts out of your head by speaking them, writing them down, or sharing them with a friend. Sometimes, as soon as you express what you're thinking, you can recognize the monster in your mind as a guest you've unintentionally been entertaining. Bringing your hidden thoughts out into the open is an excellent way to gain perspective on whether they are real.

One of the best ways to examine your thoughts is to shine the light of God's truth on them instead of focusing on the monster in your mind, however real it might seem at the moment.

> Bringing your hidden thoughts out into the open is an excellent way to gain perspective on whether they are real.

You are in a fight. We are spiritual beings, and we are in a spiritual battle. While God wants you to live fully as the person He designed you to be, other forces war against that possibility. Don't be bamboozled by thoughts that are based on nothing more than shadows of reality. To rescue the girl in you, you have to release patterns of thinking that incorrectly color how you see your world and how you choose to interact with it.

Releasing incorrect habits will take work. It won't feel comfortable, and it probably won't be easy. Rescue efforts rarely are.

But without your effort to master your thought life and wrangle the rogue notions that run around in your head, you stand to miss out on what's beautiful in your present and what's possible in your future.

Take Your Thoughts Captive

When my kids were small, they always asked me to turn on a night-light before I left their rooms and close all the doors so the monsters wouldn't come in. When I turned the light on, they weren't as afraid. They could see there weren't any monsters. The light enabled them to know their fears were unfounded and helped them to experience the freedom of thinking, feeling, and acting based on what was really true.

Now, you might be asking, "What do you mean by 'turn on the light,' and how do you do it?" First of all, coaching your thought life is something you can learn and get better at over time. Don't sweat it if you aren't good at it now. You can learn. You can grow.

The goal is to take thoughts that are negative, untrue, and destructive and replace them with thoughts that are affirming, true, and constructive. You do this by renewing your mind—transforming the way you think through ongoing acceptance of right thoughts based on what God says is true. Philippians 4:8 says, "Finally, brethren, whatever is true, whatever is honorable, whatever is right, whatever is pure, whatever is lovely, whatever is of good repute, if there is any excellence and if anything worthy of praise, dwell on these things" (NASB).

Let me show you how this works.

Let's say I found myself thinking this way: "I will never be able to accomplish my dreams."

That statement isn't true. You can shine the light of God's truth on that lie: "It is God who works in you to will and to act in order to fulfill his good purpose" (Phil. 2:13 NIV).

The truth is, as we follow God's direction in our lives, He is the one who will do the work in us so we can fulfill His purposes for us and the desires He has placed in us. That takes the pressure off our having to figure it all out, now, doesn't it?

Here's another one: "I am not enough. I'm not equipped. I don't belong."

The truth is if God put you where you are and if pleasing Him is your aim, then you *are* enough, you *are* equipped, and you *can* have victory over what you face. Second Corinthians 2:14 says, "But thanks be to God, who always leads us in triumph in Christ" (NASB).

Let's do one more together: "Since there is something wrong with my body because of illness or physical challenge, I don't have the same value as others who have their health."

The truth is you are more than your physical body. You have a unique soul, remember? God offers you the gift of the Spirit, which allows you to get better on the inside regardless of what is happening on the outside. Here's the truth according to 2 Corinthians 4:16: "So we do not lose heart. Though our outer self is wasting away, our inner self is being renewed day by day" (ESV).

If you don't know the truths of Scripture, it's your job to search them out. If you want to know what God thinks, you can discover His truth in the letter of love He's provided for you to read. He has promised that when you look for Him, you will find Him: "You will seek me and find me when you seek me with all your heart" (Jer. 29:13).

> Take thoughts that are negative, untrue, and destructive and replace them with thoughts that are affirming, true, and constructive.

Search out the truth. Write down the verses or passages that speak to your heart, and you will change your incorrect patterns of thinking over time. Inundate yourself with the truth, and that truth will become a light that shines brighter than the dark thoughts that threaten to keep you from making progress. "You will know the truth, and the truth will set you free" (John 8:32).

Don't be so busy staring into the darkness that you lose sight of the light. Even when the monster in your mind seems real and true, you must examine your thoughts in the light of God's thoughts toward you, and then believe what He says. Even if you aren't convinced, you still have to get up, cross the room, and turn on the light!

Your job now—and for the rest of your life—is to turn on the light in your mind, to embrace the truth, and to reject lies. Just because you think it, that doesn't make it true. The truth is your weapon to war with the darkness that threatens to cloud your mind.

When you choose to think right thoughts, you battle against destructive patterns of thinking that threaten to keep the girl in you from emerging valiant and victorious.

> Examine your thoughts in the light of God's thoughts toward you.

In this life, there will be moments when you feel as if you have lost the ability to breathe. There will be times when you don't know what to do. You may find yourself frozen and feel unable to move forward.

In those moments, you must choose to encourage yourself. Be your own coach. Learn to recognize the monster in your mind. Take note of destructive thoughts, then take them captive by shining on them the light of God's truth.

Reflections for the Rescue

REMEMBER

Examine your thoughts in the light of God's thoughts toward you.

REFLECT

- What thoughts do you have that steal your hope, your joy, or your motivation?
- Do you typically entertain those thoughts or fight back with truth? Why?
- What is one favorite truth from Scripture that gives you hope, stirs up joy, or motivates you to action?

RESPOND

- The next time you struggle with entertaining a destructive thought, search for a Scripture on that topic that will shine the light of truth on the monster in your mind. Keep a running list of Scriptures and build your "truth bank"—true thoughts that replace the false ones.
- Plan a good time and place to regularly get your thoughts out of your head. Write them down or share them with a friend, but examine your thoughts regularly.

Romans 12:2; Philippians 4:8; Ephesians 4:20–24;
John 1:5; John 8:12; 2 Corinthians 10:5; John 17:19.

SWIM AGAINST
THE CURRENT

Coach Your Heart

A few weeks ago a girl named Rosie approached me after church. She'd broken up with her boyfriend months before but was still struggling to be content with her life now that she was not in a relationship. Rosie told me that nothing in her life had gone right since the breakup and that everything was difficult. Her day-to-day felt like swimming against the current. She'd given up the relationship to honor God by choosing to practice celibacy, but she felt betrayed by God because she wasn't happy and was feeling miserable.

As a friend, I asked Rosie a few questions to understand where she was coming from. When I asked her about work, she said she loved her job. When I questioned her about her social life, she said she had a good group of friends and ample opportunity to get out and socialize. When I inquired about her relationship with God, she admitted she could be more consistent in her time with Him but overall felt like she was in a good place.

I looked at her and said, "So basically not *everything* in your life is problematic. There are lots of things going right in your life. You're just choosing to focus on the one thing that is not okay and let it cloud all that is okay."

Rosie had fallen into a pit that many of us fall into. We hyperfocus on one thing we don't like about our lives, and our dissatisfaction with that one area infects how we see other areas as well.

I understood Rosie's plight because I've been in her shoes. I know what it's like to be undone by the pain of a broken relationship. I remember being so encumbered by the shame of my teenage pregnancy that I let that shame color my thoughts about other experiences. That perpetuated other times I lost my footing, my sense of confidence, and my expectant and hopeful attitude in other areas of my life.

I know what it's like to be an overwhelmed single parent, not sure how to take care of my business while also taking care of my soul. I know what it's like to pour everything into my home and children, then wonder what was becoming of me as everything and everyone seemed to pass me by. I know what it's like to feel alone, forgotten, disappointed, and exhausted and to let my thoughts and emotions color how I think and feel about everything else.

But because I've been there, I've learned something.

Head-to-Heart versus Heart-to-Head

Regardless of how we feel about what's happening in our lives, we need to learn how to interpret our emotions. Sometimes emotion comes suddenly. We realize after the fact that we have fallen into a pit and are now way under the ground. But many times, feelings engulf us gradually. Drifts often begin with emotions that, like strong currents, gradually carry us away. Our choice to coach ourselves through our emotions can either perpetuate the pit we find ourselves in or prevent us from sinking further.

As I listened to Rosie express the ache in her heart, her disappointment in God, and her frustration with her life, I also heard her express a deep-seated belief that all was lost and nothing would ever get better.

I heard her express the loss of hope.

Rosie's heartache had impacted her head. The way she saw her world was affected by the breakup. She used words like always, never, everything, and nothing—words of generalization that illustrated her overarching paradigm and view of her life. I heard in her voice and saw in her body language that she had lost her motivation to fight. She was overcome by waves of emotion and had sunk far enough beneath the surface that she was unable to breathe.

When our souls are impacted by pain, it affects the feelings we experience in our hearts. It also connects our experiences with our thoughts, and those thoughts feed the root system of our beliefs.

If you don't believe you can win, you won't feel like fighting. If you don't feel like fighting, you won't even bother showing up for the battle. And if you don't show up for the battle, you've become your own worst enemy, because now *you* are the reason why winning is not even a possibility.

> Our choice to coach ourselves through our emotions can either perpetuate the pit we find ourselves in or prevent us from sinking further.

My job is to convince you that winning is possible.

One of the biggest time-wasters in my life has been my lack of confidence that winning is possible. When I felt rejected, emotionally bankrupt, and heartbroken, I lost my will to fight.

I quit showing up.

I stopped trying.

I became my own worst enemy, using my words to tear myself down as if expecting less of my life would make getting less out of my life any easier. I let my heart infect my thoughts, which in turn reinforced emotions that influenced my incorrect choices.

It took me a long time to learn the lesson that I want to share with you now.

It is your job to coach your heart. You've got to keep tabs on your emotions. When you notice your feelings trying to take you farther than it would be wise to go, you must know how to care for your heart while coaching yourself back to emotional stability.

You are not the sum total of how you feel.

Some of your most difficult battles will be the tug-of-war between your head and your heart. Your heart cannot be the primary factor which determines how you live your life. I hate to be the one to break it to you, but your heart will lie to you and keep you from clearly seeing the truths you should act on. As Jeremiah 17:9 says, "The heart is deceitful above all things, and desperately sick; who can understand it?" (ESV).

> You are not the sum total of how you feel.

Emotions are real, and while they should inform, they shouldn't be in charge. If you choose to follow your heart and go with the flow of your feelings, your feelings just might pull you under.

To let your heart dictate your actions is to go dancing in a minefield. Your emotions are not equipped to lead you well.

I told you earlier in our journey together to pay attention to what you feel—to honor your emotions by recognizing the purpose of both joy and pain, and to honor your soul by making room for joy and making the effort to walk fully through pain to healing. There is a time for that.

But now I want to tell you to look deeply into what your emotions are doing to you. If your emotions are dragging you down, it is your job to fight back. It is your job to reverse direction if you're feelings are dictating what you're doing. Heart-to-head should become head-to-heart.

Emotions Guide, Not Govern

Let's return to Rosie's story. I realized that this young woman was buried underneath deep emotional pain, so I gave her words back to her in order for her to examine them.

"Rosie, you said that nothing in your life is going right, but you also told me you love your job and you have a good group of friends. Is nothing really going right in your life, or is your heart telling your head a lie?

"You said everything in your life is difficult, yet you have a family who loves you and a relationship with God that you're working on. Is everything really hard and difficult, or are you giving disappointment in one area of your life too much credit?"

As I talked with this young woman, it occurred to me she didn't realize she'd been acting as her own worst enemy. She didn't see that she'd allowed her feelings to carry her away. She didn't understand the importance of using her mouth to speak life to her soul the same way she would speak to a friend. She was gladly walking in step with her hurt, never stopping to wonder whether she actually desired to go to the place her emotions were leading her.

Part of coaching yourself through self-talk is asking yourself questions. Keep asking yourself the five W's—who, what, when, why, and where—and throw in an occasional how for good measure. When your emotions are running away and taking your head and sensibilities with them, fight for the girl in you by being willing to do the hard work of heart examination.

Sometimes that work might be too much for you to do yourself.

It's okay if you need help from a friend or a licensed counselor to work through issues and identify appropriate responses based on healthy thoughts and beliefs. And it's okay if you can't get to the root of things in one conversation. Swimming against the current is hard work. And the heart moves slowly sometimes.

There is nothing wrong with understanding your heart, experiencing the emotions of the heart, and caring for your heart. You just can't live your life acting on the demands of the heart. If you allow your heart to lead your actions, you just might act in ways that hurt yourself or others.

The last time I felt like I'd received a punch in the gut was when one of my children hurt me deeply. I felt as if a dagger had been thrust through my heart. My first reaction was pain, but the close second was anger.

I'm sad to say I felt that anger for a long time. I coddled it. I nurtured it. I acted on it with passive-aggressive behavior of which I am not proud. I remember thinking it would take too much energy to do anything other than that. My heart ruled my head.

And I lost time.

But one day I heard myself say something out loud to my husband that revealed the toxicity of my heart, words that clearly exhibited how much my heart had infected my thoughts and, in turn, my actions.

I was shocked to realize how far my emotions had carried me.

At this point, I decided to work through that hurt, expressing some thoughts on paper and others verbally. I asked myself questions boring deeply into the root of my responses and the reasons for my reactions. When I struggled to find the answers, I asked my husband and a close friend to help me do the work.

Why was I angry? What had begun my emotional downward spiral? When did it start? What had made it worse? What expectation did I have that hadn't been met? Why was I bothered when I discovered the depth of my anger? What did I need to do to address that conviction?

By using my words—verbal and written—to talk to myself and others about the source of my harmful emotions, I was able to isolate the root of my hurt and anger: a desire to be appreciated for all the sacrifices I'd made over the years.

But I didn't stop there. I rehearsed the truth of the love I believed in my head. I recalled God's love for me and His forgiveness. I remembered how unlovable and how hurtful I'd been to others in my life, people who continued to love me despite the pain I caused them. Slowly but surely, I talked myself down off the ledge and worked through my emotional response. Remembering God's love for me helped me to decide—apart from my emotions—how best to show love and forgiveness toward my child who had hurt me.

I learned how to feel without letting my emotions rule.

Feel fully, but don't let your heart lead you to hurt yourself or others. Process your emotions. Work through the hard stuff by yourself or with someone you trust. But never forget: emotions can guide you, but they shouldn't govern you.

Show Up Like You Are Meant to Be There

People wouldn't know it, but many times when I get in front of a group to speak, I'm a ball of nerves. I wonder if the people in the audience will benefit from anything I have to say, or if they'll fall asleep while I'm talking because they think I'm boring as all get out.

My audience doesn't see me backstage, pacing and trying to remember my main points. They don't notice me when I'm sitting in the front row, squeezing my hands together in an effort to calm myself down before I speak. They aren't aware of how deeply I breathe as I try to slow my racing heart.

They don't know I'm a ball of nerves, because I've learned something. I've learned how important it is for me to rule my emotions instead of letting my emotions rule me. While I don't always do it perfectly, I under-stand the importance of not wearing every emotion on my sleeve and talking to my heart based on what my head knows to be true.

I've also learned the art of showing up.

As a person who struggles with insecurity, I sometimes find myself feeling unworthy, ill-equipped, or undeserving. But I know that the way I feel isn't always the barometer of what is true.

It is my job to show up in every single moment of my life as if I'm meant to be there. I can't always wait until I feel powerful or confident. Coaching my heart

> **The way you feel isn't always the barometer of what is true.**

means moving ahead in my weakness, doing my best in spite of my fears or feelings, acting as if what should be actually is. Sometimes that means I fake it till I make it, based on what I know to be true. I do the best I can with what I know until I know to do better. Showing up also means:

- Acting cheerfully when I don't feel cheerful.
- Serving when I don't think I have much of a servant's heart.
- Smiling when my children come into the room, even though I want to scream, "Give me five minutes, please!"
- Maintaining a posture of support toward my husband when I'm wondering why in the world he made a certain decision.
- Walking into a room with my head held high even when I know nobody in the room knows my name.
- Applying for a job even though I'm not confident I'll get it.
- Introducing myself when I realize someone else won't do it for me.
- Being brave enough to do what pleases God when I'm used to doing what pleases others.
- Breathing deeply to slow my racing heart even as I walk to the front of a room.

If God has provided an opportunity for you, show up like you're supposed to be there.

Coaching your heart means you don't operate on your feelings alone. You don't mindlessly go with the flow but instead choose to swim against the current when necessary. Understand your emotions. Deal with them appropriately. But don't let your emotions have the last word. Look at your heart. Listen to your heart. Learn your heart, but don't let it lead.

Reflections for the Rescue

REMEMBER

You are not the sum total of how you feel.

REFLECT

- Has your heart ever led you astray? Did you know the truth, or did you ignore it?
- Are you an emotional "sharer" or an emotional "stuffer"? What could be helpful and hurtful about each?
- How best do you process your emotions? Alone or with a friend? Talking it out or writing it down? Slow and easy or fast and furious?

RESPOND

The next time you are experiencing a strong emotion, hold it in the light of truth. Ask yourself the five W's—who, what, when, why, and where—and evaluate how you feel in light of God's Word. Then act on truth.

Psalms 26:2; Jeremiah 17:9; John 8:32;
Ephesians 6:14; 1 John 1:5–9.

PUT A LITTLE SUGAR ON IT

Coach Your Hands

I love to plan. I love brainstorming, making lists, and writing goals. I've tried many planning systems and project management tools, and my phone is full of apps that are supposed to help me get my act together too (#appjunkie). There's just one problem. I don't always couple my extensive planning with actions that will bring my plans to life.

It's not enough to talk a good game if you want to see real change in your life. You also have to be willing to walk a good game.

There's this trick I've discovered that helps me to quickly drill down with laser precision on the actions I can take to propel me forward.

I ask myself this question: What can I do in the next ninety days that will have an impact and help me to make progress? What can I do to move the needle in my life?

Recently, I decided I wanted to move the needle in my marriage. I figured I could stand to be a little sweeter to my husband and cultivate a deeper connection in our relationship. Now, I'm not mean or anything. The problem is I'm just not the sweet type. Thinking about becoming a touchy-feely kind of wife makes me cringe, and the idea seems totally overwhelming. In this instance, though, I thought about what I might do in ninety days that could move me toward sweetness without making me feel as if I were drowning in sugar.

Ya'll, I love my husband. God knows I do (said in my best *The Color Purple* voice). But reaching out to hold his hand hasn't always been easy for me. My husband will tell you that even the first time he reached to hold my hand when we were dating, I quickly let it go. Let's just say I have hand-holding issues.

But since I'd decided to move the needle in my marriage and put a little sugar on it by showing my husband affection, I also decided to act by coaching my hands into doing what I wanted them to do to get the result I wanted: seeing my husband's face light up.

I've talked to you already about the importance of doing one thing. Well, I've found that upping it to three things doesn't require much more energy, and there's way less pressure because you've got ninety days to work on 'em.

I decided that over the next ninety days I would put a little sugar on it by not only reaching to hold his hand more often but also saying "yes, love" every now and then and complimenting him more than I normally do. Now, if I'd said I intended to be a more loving and doting wife, that goal would have made me want to throw up. But focusing on three specific actions over time didn't seem as daunting.

Sure, I could work on taking action over the standard habit-forming period of twenty-one days, but when what you're looking to change is not so much a daily habit as making large shifts in your priorities or purpose, I think three things over the course of ninety days is just what the doctor ordered.

1. Identify Your Destination

Every so often, I sit down and do a brain dump. I write down everything, from the mundane tasks I need to do the next day to the dreams I have for my future. Once I've emptied my brain, I examine both my paper and my heart to separate the things that are urgent and necessary from those bigger goals and desires that require focus over time in order to see real change.

While my brain dump does help me organize my thoughts about different areas of my life, I mainly use it as a tool to identify choices I need to make to move the needle. I look at that list and pray over that list and ask God to help me separate the urgent and right-now from the important and long-term.

Think about the areas in your life that you'd like to change. Maybe you want to do a better job of nurturing your soul by reading more, investing in meaningful relationships, or spending a few hours without your kids every now and then to recharge. Maybe you need to deal with an ache in your soul or pursue a path to healing. Maybe you want to follow a dream, develop personally or professionally, improve your health, or better your marriage.

Listen to your life.

What is it telling you? What expectations for yourself are not being met? What does God expect out of your life that you are not producing? What will matter most to you five years from now? Ten years from now? Are you doing what it takes to have what you desire?

Listen to your life.

Identify what matters most to you. Separate those goals and desires from the everyday concerns that can crowd them out. Thinking about your life propels you from owning your story to moving toward a new story, a new narrative for the girl in you.

2. Pick Three Things

After identifying the areas that need your long-term attention, take one of those areas and identify three steps you can take in the next ninety days that will help you move closer to your destination.

If you want to go back to school, the cost, preparation, and commitment can be overwhelming, but if in the next ninety days you only need to visit a school, fill out an application, and visit with a counselor, you can do that.

If you want to improve your marriage, that idea can seem vague, but if you decide in the next ninety days to say "I love you" more, make his favorite meals more often, and do at least one thing that feeds his need for your support and respect, that's manageable.

If you are terribly shy and want to work on your interactions with others, in ninety days you can invite a coworker to lunch, offer to pray with a neighbor, and find a Toastmasters group in your area where you can improve your communication skills in a safe, supportive environment.

The goal is to move closer, not to arrive. No pressure here.

3. Focus on Three Things

Now it's time to decide how you'll give those three things priority in your life. Build your schedule around them. Make time for them. Spend less time on other things so you can spend more time on the three things you've decided will make a difference in your story.

If you commit to taking three small steps, the energy you use will motivate you to take still more small steps. And that will give you even more energy to keep taking action.

Your energy will breed momentum, and your momentum will breed visualization.

Now, I know that totally sounds super self-helpish. So let me say it another way: "Faith is the substance of things hoped for, the evidence of things not seen" (Heb. 11:1 KJV).

When you choose to operate with actions of evidence (what you do) based on what you hope for (who you are), you are operating in faith.

There you have it. God said it first—and more succinctly, I might add.

When you focus on just three things—and take action on them—you will raise your self-respect, teach yourself that you can be trusted, and build the confidence that you are indeed capable of more.

4. Create Checkpoints

If you make a goal but don't periodically review it, you will lose sight of it. That's the way it is with us humans. We drift if we don't occasionally check to make sure we're staying on course.

As soon as you decide on the three steps you plan to take, also decide on a timeframe for checking your progress.

After hammering out my top priorities, I try to review my areas of focus on a monthly basis to see how I'm doing. This keeps me from going too long without putting thought into the most important things in my life. You may want to review your "big three" monthly like I do, or maybe you'll choose to do it weekly or even daily. The frequency should be a function of what your three steps are and how often you need the reminder to work on them.

If there is a change I need to make in my spiritual life, I aim to check in daily. I've found that if I'm not thinking and praying every day about what needs to happen, things can fall apart fast. I want everything I do to flow out of my relationship with God, and that means He and I need to have a face-to-face every day.

Maybe you need to hop on the bathroom scale every week. Maybe annually, you set a goal for the number of books you want to read or Bible verses you want to memorize, and you evaluate your progress down that list every quarter. Maybe you need to aim for a regular date night with your husband or spend more one-on-one time with your children or with certain friends. Maybe once a month, you need a few hours to look yourself in the eye and see how you're really doing.

If you want to honor the girl in you and the life she is supposed to live, you need to check up on her regularly.

5. Course-Correct

It does you no good to identify where you're going, pick three steps to get yourself there, prioritize, and check in, if you don't course-correct when you realize you're not on track.

This is where discipline comes in.

We typically get off track because we didn't feel like doing whatever was necessary to keep working toward our destination. Then, instead of recalibrating when we realize we've fallen off the wagon, we sit in the ditch and feel sorry for ourselves.

I'm guilty of this. I will spew thoughts and words of self-pity, bemoaning how much harder my life is than everyone else's and how I'll never get it together. Instead of using the frustration as energy to propel me back up and onto the road, I wallow in regret and sadness.

> If you want to honor the girl in you and the life she is supposed to live, you need to check up on her regularly.

Discipline propels you back into motion when you feel like sitting still. Discipline makes you look critically at your life when you feel like pretending that nothing happened, that you didn't make a mistake, or that you're incapable of living out the life you've been given.

Be brave enough to look at your life.

Where have you gotten off track—and why?

It's common knowledge that people with long-term weight-loss success watch what they eat, keep an eye on the scale, and observe how their pants slide over their hips. And they don't just look at what they eat or how much they eat; they also pay attention to *why* they eat. They learn the triggers that lead them to reach for sugar or salt. They recognize how emotions like loneliness or sadness push them toward edible comfort, how stress tempts them to nibble in the afternoon or late at night, and how their monthly cycle can suddenly make them ravenous for all the wrong things. I can't tell you the number of times I've caught myself looking in the pantry or the refrigerator out of boredom. *Now where is that pint of ice cream I hid from my family?*

You need to know your triggers. Know what helps you to stay focused. Know what makes it hard and then adjust accordingly.

Whatever your finish line might be, you must consistently keep tabs on whether you're staying on track. Then, if you realize you've drifted, do the hard, disciplined work of correcting your course. Recognize your poor choices, but don't lament over them too long. Get back to the work of getting your finances together, improving your marriage, growing in your relationship with God, extending forgiveness, being present with your family, or getting healthy.

> Be brave enough to look at your life.

Your finish line is waiting on you.

And if you find yourself stopping for a break or even running backward, it's not too late to get your act together and keep moving toward the finish line.

You can coach yourself toward the girl in you.

Identify your areas of focus and what steps you will take to move toward them. Decide how you will give those three things priority. Build your schedule around them. Make time for them. Do less of other things so you can do more of the three things you've decided will make a difference in your story.

Check in regularly to assess your progress and, if you've gotten off track, do whatever is necessary to get it together and move on.

Ninety days.

Three things.

Prioritize.

Check in.

Correct.

That's it.

Oh! And when you decide on your three things, share them with someone else who can hold you accountable for doing whatever it is you said you were going to do. Tell that person what you plan to do and the date by which you plan to do it.

Focus on taking practical steps that will move the needle in your life and propel you. Coach your hands into action. Reach when it's uncomfortable. Work through your issues while still moving forward. Never doubt that all of your actions matter.

And if needed, put a little sugar on it and get going.

Reflections for the Rescue

REMEMBER

Listen to your life.

REFLECT

- Listen to your life. What hopes do you have for it?
- What about your life would you like to change in the next year?
- Our thoughts and our feelings can inform us, but they don't get anything done. What action needs to accompany your hopes and desires?

RESPOND

Walk through the ninety-day exercise presented in this chapter. Identify a goal you would like to work toward. Pick three things you can do to work toward that goal. Make those tasks a priority and decide on a point in the future when you will review your progress.

Hebrews 11:1; Romans 12:2; Philippians 4:8–9;
John 8:32; Ephesians 4:20–24; John 1:5; John 8:12;
1 John 1:5–9; Ephesians 6:14.

PART 6

CHOOSE YOUR LIFE

For whatever it's worth: it's never too late to be
whoever you want to be. I hope you live a life
you're proud of, and if you find that you're not,
I hope you have the strength to start over.

—*F. Scott Fitzgerald*

I would like to be remembered as a
person who wanted to be free . . .
so other people would also be free.

—*Rosa Parks*

PRACTICE AN ATTITUDE OF GRATITUDE

Choose Celebration

My husband, Jessie, and I were in the middle of a hard season. We were meeting with a therapist who specialized in helping patients and their families navigate the difficulties that follow a major health crisis.

Six months earlier, Jessie had suffered a stroke. What followed were months of doctor's appointments, therapy visits, and changing dynamics in our home and in our marriage.

He was different.

I was different.

We were forever changed by that event.

The therapist, Ms. Kate, sat across from us asking questions to assess Jessie's progress after the stroke and how that progress was impacting our home. Her job was to help both of us understand the maze of medical care that was now a permanent fixture of daily life and to help us make sense of it all.

We were searching for our new normal.

At a certain point in the conversation, Ms. Kate paused, sighed deeply, looked both of us in the eye, and said, "You know what you all's problem is? You don't celebrate."

A bit taken aback, I searched for something to say in response but didn't get a chance to speak because she kept talking.

"Jessie has had a major health challenge, but it's been six months. He has experienced a remarkable recovery thus far, and while things aren't perfect or all the way back to normal, they're so much better than they were. You both have had your own set of challenges, but don't limit yourself to focusing on the challenges alone."

We both just sat there looking at her.

She continued, "You must decide to celebrate your small victories and practice gratitude for every blessing along the way. You owe it to yourselves to do that."

I've never forgotten those words.

I'd never thought of myself as someone who doesn't celebrate. I celebrate all the normal stuff, you know? Birthdays. Graduations. Christmas. I'm usually at church to ring in the New Year, and I try my best to attend all the weddings I've been invited to.

But celebrate small victories? Show gratitude for seemingly insignificant, everyday things?

I don't think I'm a natural in that department.

I'm a realist.

At least, that's what I like to tell myself.

In reality, I tend toward pessimism. A pragmatist to the nth degree, I like to feel prepared for anything negative that might happen, even if a more positive outcome is a possibility. My thought process is that if I expect the worst possible result, nothing will catch me off guard and anything better will be cause for celebration when I'm sure it's safe to do so.

In addition to my tendency not to notice and give thanks for the small yet beautiful things in my life, after being in my husband's presence when he experienced his stroke, I was scared.

I worried a lot.

Every day, I wondered if he would have another one. I didn't have the energy to find something for which to be grateful because I was spending all my energy waiting for the other shoe to drop.

You know, so that when it did, I'd be prepared.

On top of the emotional and mental weight of my concerns, a celebratory attitude seemed to elude me because of practical matters—calls to the insurance company, doctor visits, the usual duties that come with a house full of kids. It just was too much.

Let's be real here. Sometimes you don't want to celebrate the life you have because the life you have is not the life you want. It's a whole lot easier to settle for low expectations and probable disappointment than to show appreciation for what lies directly in front of you and to expend the energy to hope for change.

But here's the thing. Until the moment Ms. Kate bluntly shared her thoughts, I'd never thought of celebration as necessary to real living. I didn't see celebration for what it really is—a tool to see beyond my problems to what is possible, a choice to value my life through gratitude and thanksgiving, and an opportunity to honor, observe, and remember the unique beauty in my story.

Celebration Gives Hope

Celebration is a tool that helps you continue to hope, and it is through hope that we stay open to possibility.

Hope is the belief that things will work out for the better. It is a driving force that keeps us going even when things look dim. When you stop celebrating the important moments of your life, you suffocate hope and close yourself off to the very things you desire.

I desired many more days of enjoying life with Jessie and seeing him enjoy life with our children, family, and friends. But as I focused on the hard work needed to make my way back—our way back—to a place of normal, I was missing moments to enjoy along the way. I was talking about hope but not living out hope. I was hesitant to embrace my right now because I was working so hard for my later.

But after that conversation with the therapist, I've been challenged to live differently, and as I learn what it means to hope and celebrate in the present, I've learned how beautiful a gift celebration can be.

When you celebrate, you look back with gratitude at where you've been and what you've done. And you also look forward with expectation to all the possibilities in your future.

And so I made small changes. On the way to the doctor's office, I added time for Jessie and I to stop for a lunch date. As my husband's memory improved, I squealed with delight over the incremental progress. And a little later in our journey, I went out for a cup of coffee by myself, to celebrate my ability to do so without concern.

> You are a remarkable person, and your life is an ongoing remarkable event worthy of being celebrated along the way.

Celebration is more than recognition. Celebration is the way you mark the moments of your life. It involves heartfelt experiences that create lasting memories. Those memories are the building blocks for your perception of your existence on this earth.

You might be good at acknowledging a remarkable person or event in a culminating moment, but *you* are also a remarkable person, and your life is an ongoing remarkable event worthy of being celebrated along the way.

Celebration Helps You Thrive

The last time I lost weight—'cuz you know I've been in a tug-of-war with the same thirty to forty pounds all my life—I was mortified when a friend announced at a large gathering the amount of weight I'd lost.

It wasn't the sharing of the number that was problematic. I make no secret of my journey of weight loss, and I knew my friend simply wanted to acknowledge my achievement. Discomfort enveloped me because my friend celebrated as if I'd won.

And I didn't think I had.

I wasn't ready to claim victory because I hadn't reached my goal—the ultimate goal, the number on the scale I'd determined as the point at which I would shout for joy. I was treating my goal weight as if it were the only victory to celebrate, as if every other pound I'd lost didn't matter.

But what I didn't understand is that when I treat my incremental steps forward as if they matter, I'm telling myself that I'm capable of success. And that self-talk makes a difference, as subconscious as the narrative may be.

Small successes have this funny way of breeding more of the same.

Because I didn't understand this principle, I got really good at stifling self-appreciation and gratitude, almost as good as I got at rejecting the celebration offered to me by others. When someone told me that I looked good or that they were proud of my accomplishment, I was quick to dismiss their celebration by making some snarky, clothed-in-comedy statement.

"Let's hope I can keep it off."

"Honey, if I lose all this weight and gain it back, I'm not ever doing this again. It's too hard. I'd rather be fat and happy."

"Girl, you know me—going up and down the scale is what I do."

Do you ever wave off the compliments or encouragement of others? Please stop. You are rejecting a gift.

If the art of celebration and gratefulness isn't cultivated, sarcasm, disappointment, entitlement, and negativity quickly sprout in its place.

Your refusal to celebrate is not a neutral activity. It hurts you.

When we dismiss our progress, we miss the opportunity to tell ourselves we are capable and adept at achieving a favorable outcome. And we unintentionally shame our girl into taking two steps backward.

Once you begin to celebrate your small achievements, you begin to accept that you are capable of doing it again. So set small goals. Aspire. Dream. Live with intention, even if you limit your ideas or plans to the next ninety days. That will give you something to aim for and a moment you can mark with thankfulness, acknowledgment, and maybe a tiny bit of personal partying—you know, with sparkling grape juice or something.

I recently listened to a podcast where Lisa Nichols, a motivational speaker, expressed my problem with celebration and my resulting difficulty in moving forward: "Don't get attached to the number of times you fall down. Get attached to the number of times you get back up again."

The moment I heard her words, I knew I'd slowly become attached to falling down. Instead of celebrating the times I've restarted, tried again, or inched forward, I'd developed the habit of looking for defeat because it somehow seemed easier to find. But it was only easier to find because I'd had lots of practice looking for it.

Don't subject yourself only to the rhythm and routine of life and leave out the reward of living with a grateful heart for each and every step you take. Focus on what you've accomplished, rather than on a long, overwhelming list of what you've still got to do.

> Focus on what you've accomplished, rather than on a long, overwhelming list of what you've still got to do.

When you choose to celebrate and be thankful, you shine a light on your small victories, which nurtures and sets the stage for more of the same.

So let's mark our moments. Take notice of the milestones, achievements, and the good in the everyday. In so doing, we will encourage more of the same.

Celebrate that birthday or anniversary. Reward yourself when you reach a goal. Look for the little things in each day for which you can be grateful.

And if you see me looking good in a bangin' pair of skinny jeans, tell me so. Then remind me to just say thank you. I'll do my best to smile and take the compliment.

Celebration Is Good for You

I am the crazy lady on the elliptical machine at the gym.

I plug in my headphones, and instantaneously I somehow believe I'm the only one who can see me.

I move my feet to the beat of whatever song comes next on my playlist. I clap my hands and probably sing out loud, but I wouldn't know because I can't hear myself really. If the song gets really good and the Spirit "gets ahold of me," I can be seen waving my hands in the air.

Church.

I have church on the elliptical machine.

And once I get off the machine, walk out of the gym, and drive off to begin my day, you can't tell me *nothin'*.

I'm energized.

I'm hyped up.

I feel powerful and capable.

This is all possibly due to the endorphins I charged up while spinning my legs madly around in circle.

Hold on to your hat here. I'm about to go scientifically rogue on ya.

Endorphins are neurotransmitters that flood in when we exercise, laugh, cry, smile, play, and . . .

Wait for it . . .

Celebrate.

Think about the last time you attended some kind of celebration—a wedding, a birthday party, a graduation, or a New Year's get-together. Did you smile? Was there laughter involved? Did you go home with your soul full, even if you were dog tired?

Well, your brain gave your body the gift of a burst of endorphins! Endorphins are known to relieve pain and induce feelings of pleasure or euphoria. They reduce stress and improve your mood, which also improves your outlook on your life.

Endorphins have friends, too. Dopamine is released when you achieve, so your choice to celebrate small victories means you get a hit every time you achieve something or anticipate achievement. Serotonin is released in response to assigned value. When others celebrate you or acknowledge you in some way, you benefit from a neurotransmitter designed to regulate your mood. Oxytocin is the bonding hormone that increases when it's time for a mother to nurse her baby. It also increases or decreases proportionately to when someone you care about expresses deep gratitude for your friendship.

There is a physiological connection between what you think, how you feel, and what you do. Proverbs 15:13 says, "A joyful heart makes a cheerful face, but when the heart is sad, the spirit is broken" (NASB). Celebration affects your outlook on life and impacts your physiological responses to what's happening to you. It makes you feel better.

When you choose to celebrate, you see the world differently, and not just because you're being an irritating, overly positive Pollyanna. With your decision to celebrate and give thanks, you instruct your body to lower your stress level, your brain to have a more positive outlook, and your heart to be more deeply engaged in meaningful relationships.

Celebration is good for you.

Even if you hope your world gets "gooder" over time, don't miss the opportunity you have to mark the moments of your life with celebration and an attitude of gratitude right now.

Celebration Is Easy

My heart understood more deeply this concept of celebration when I watched Sheryl Sandburg, the author of *Lean In*, give a commencement speech just a year after the unexpected and sudden death of her husband, Dave. She shared that a friend asked her to think, even in her grieving, how much worse things could be.

"Worse?" she said. "Are you kidding me? How could things be worse?"

I don't blame her. I might have punched that friend right in the chest.

But then Sheryl's friend talked about how much worse things could have been. Instead of Dave dying alone, which was one of the hardest parts of Sheryl's grieving, what if he'd had the cardiac arrest while he was driving and their two children were in the car with him? In that moment, Sheryl realized that even in her grief, she still had something to be grateful for. In that moment, gratitude overtook some of her grief.

As often as you can, no matter how bad you think things are, give thanks. Find something—anything—to express gratitude for, and make it a point to take notice of your life and honor your existence with small celebrations along the way.

Don't wait until the grand arrival at your desired destination.

Spend time regularly—daily, if possible—noting what's right in your life. Write those things down. Say them out loud to yourself in the mirror. Spend more time thanking God for what He's done than expressing frustration for what you're still waiting on Him to do. And every now and then

> **No matter how bad you think things are, give thanks.**

- Break out the china.
- Meet up with friends.
- Do something that makes you laugh.

- Go to the party even if you don't feel like it.
- Spend time counting your blessings.
- Make celebration your new normal.

And be purposeful about it. Look for ways to celebrate and express gratitude for who you are, where you've been, and where you're going.

Celebration is the way you honor the girl in you. Your celebration of her validates her existence and her accomplishments each step along the way. Your choice to applaud her efforts tells her that she matters not because she has arrived but because she *is*.

When you celebrate her, you encourage her to bravely offer her gifts to the world. And when she does, you just might realize that the life she wants is the life she already has.

Reflections for the Rescue

REMEMBER

Celebration is the way you mark the moments of your life.

REFLECT

- Does celebration come naturally to you? Why or why not?
- When do you take time to celebrate? Do you only celebrate major milestones like birthdays, anniversaries, and special occasions, or do you celebrate the everyday?
- What could celebrating your everyday look like?

RESPOND

Spend time today noting what's right in your life. As a part of your reflection, thank God for what's right in your life. Practice gratitude.

Psalm 95:2; Colossians 4:2; Colossians 3:17;
Luke 15:11–24; Exodus 12:14; Nehemiah 8:9–10;
1 Chronicles 29:20–22; Psalm 100.

CHAPTER 27

RUN YOUR RACE

Choose Freedom

As I mentioned before, I'm a slow runner. I mean *s-l-o-w*. I hesitate to even refer to myself as a runner because I don't think someone who moves as slowly as I do should even be classified as such, especially when I am so-called running and one of those power walkers passes me by. I'm not making that up. It's happened more than once.

So why I attempted to run a marathon, God only knows.

My first marathon—and probably my last—was on a looped course. All the participants had to run to a midway point and turn around. For the first part of the race, I felt pretty accomplished. I was keeping my pace, and, with a high level of energy and excitement, I had pep in my step and a smile on my face.

That ended abruptly when I looked up and saw the *real* runners, headed in the opposite direction on the other side of the street. Those freakishly fast people were going to reach the finish line before I even reached the halfway mark.

And to make matters worse, I really wanted to quit when the "walker lady" passed me. You know, the speed-walker woman who swings her hips like there is no tomorrow and pumps her arms like she is marching in the army on fast-forward? She passed me and smiled. I think I smiled back, but as soon as she passed me, I rolled my eyes out of exasperation.

What in the name of all that is fair and good?!

Embarrassed.

Humiliated.

Demotivated.

My first marathon almost killed me. It also almost killed my will, my determination, and my self-confidence.

The truth is death-by-running didn't just happen during that marathon. Many times, I've found myself out with real runners (or speed walkers) and wanting to quit simply because I'm usually in the back and have to watch person after person pass me by. Compared to my molasses-like movement, everyone else seems to glide over the pavement like quick-pouring maple syrup on pancakes. (Food, it always comes back to food.) It seems as though others are able to do effortlessly what it appears to take every cell in my body to barely accomplish. But here's what I've learned: Comparison can kill. It can put you in virtual chains and keep you locked down in a cage you build for yourself with your own words and thoughts.

The Problem with Comparison

When we compare ourselves with others, we nurture a lack of respect for our own journey. We look at the lives of other people and construct opinions of them—and ourselves—based on what we see. The problem is we're never operating with full intel.

> Comparison can kill.

We don't know someone's whole story. People are really good at editing their lives, leaving out what they don't want to show and spotlighting what they're comfortable revealing. We all know from social media that people share more of what's right than what's wrong in their lives. Consequently, we contrast what we can see—much of it edited and online—with our own experiences, comparing the best of others' narratives with the worst of our own stories.

I love this quote by Steven Furtick: "One reason we struggle with insecurity: we're comparing our behind-the-scenes with everyone else's highlight reel."[18] Now, that there is real truth.

When you and I compare ourselves with others, we engage in an activity that doesn't do anything to help us get where we want to go. We waste energy and emotions on something that takes away from us instead of building us up. When we engage in comparing ourselves with others, we're fighting a battle we're bound to lose.

Don't ask me how I know. I'm sad to say that I've spent more time than I care to admit wishing my life were as easy as someone else's appeared to be, that I had the money they seemed to have or the talents they'd been given.

Instead of practicing regret for what you're not, enjoy the beauty of who you are.

Not only should you conquer your tendency to compare yourself with others, you have to. The health of your soul and your mind depends on it.

Conquering Comparison

Know who and what you value. When you compare, you are in effect weighing your value against the value of someone else. You juxtapose one of God's masterpieces with another. To conquer comparison, you must believe in your value, a value that exists because *you* exist. You must know what represents value in your life and measure yourself against the standard *you* have set. Get quiet, let your soul breathe, and identify what represents value in your life, then make your own goals your benchmarks.

I place a high value on sharing my home with other people. Lots of people. It brings me joy to have others spending time with me in my space, hanging out, eating food, and sleeping on my sofas when necessary. I have the space in my older, country home to do this. This value means when I catch myself feeling some kind of way about my girlfriend's brand-new, supermodern but small apartment in the city, I can quickly reign in that comparison because there's no need for me to want something that would keep me from having the experiences I value.

Be sure not to minimize things that matter to you in light of things that seem to matter to others. If it brings you joy to make quilts, don't let someone who makes designer clothes for a living make you feel crazy about the endeavor that brings you delight. If someone loves New York City but you can't get enough of life on the ranch, no matter. Sit on the porch and watch your man wrangle cattle. The Pioneer Woman does just that. Lean into your life with your whole heart. Home is where the heart is anyway.

Practice gratitude. Gratitude is the practice of being thankful and showing appreciation. When you focus on what's right in your world, you limit the power of what's wrong to steal your joy. The more you see what's beautiful in your life, the less what's outside your life will matter.

Take the energy and emotion you would spend thinking about what other people have or are doing, and instead spend that time and energy being grateful for what you have and can do today. Gratitude for your own circumstances and accomplishments also frees you to appreciate the accomplishments of others.

Give grace to yourself and encouragement to others. Whenever you find yourself in the comparison trap, give yourself grace. No one has it all together all of the time. Give yourself a break. Don't be your worst enemy. Be your best friend. What would you tell a friend who is in the middle of the struggle? Tell yourself the same thing. Out loud if you have to. Who cares whether anyone thinks you're crazy if talking out loud to yourself helps keep you sane?

Give encouragement to others when you find yourself feeling the most in knots. Giving of any kind builds your self-esteem because it puts you in a proactive position instead of a reactive one. A compliment paid to someone else can have the effect of freeing you.

Pay attention. Pay attention to those moments and situations when you tend to compare yourself with others. Learn to recognize the feelings or thoughts that accompany the habit, and be ready to conquer the comparison that threatens to steal your joy. Redirect your emotional energy into thoughts and actions that build up instead of tearing down.

Comparison is a habit. That means you can choose not to practice it. There is nothing good about practicing an activity that only results in feelings of competition, envy, or strife.

The problem is many of us don't even know we're practicing the habit of comparison. That's why it's so important to take notice of when you do. Notice when you feel bad because you see something good happening in someone else's life. Notice when you feel inferior in the presence of certain people or in certain circumstances. When you feel the emotions of jealousy, envy, or insecurity rising up, immediately practice new habits—remembering your value, finding something to be grateful for, giving yourself grace to run at your pace, giving a compliment or encouraging word to another (even if you have to force the words to come out of your mouth).

> Comparison is a habit. That means you can choose not to practice it.

Live intentionally. Let's be honest for a second. Sometimes we struggle with comparison because we see in someone else's life what we could have had in our own had we lived with more diligence, focus, or discipline. We want what someone else has, but we haven't been willing to do what it takes to get it or keep it. We want someone else's product but may not have been willing to go through the process to get it.

When you find yourself comparing for that reason, don't settle for ruminating over what someone else has achieved or regret what you could have had. Be willing to coach yourself. Be intentional about learning and maintaining the attitudes and actions that will get you where you want to go, and move from where you are now to where you think you could have been. Never waste time sulking when you can spend that time in activities that can improve your situation.

Focus on an audience of one. Take the time to figure out what the girl in you desires and what God desires for her too. Act as if only one standing ovation matters for the way you live your life.

God will not ask you about how you lived in comparison with other people. He will only want to know that you did what you could with what you had, trusting Him for the process of progress and *the* answer only He can provide.

Listen, my friend. We don't all run the same pace. We don't all run in the same race. The art of running your race well starts with the recognition that you are running *your* race. In that knowledge there is freedom. There is no one like you, either in years gone by or in years to come, who will have your exact stride, path, scenery, or destination.

Freedom comes when you realize the person running next to you can't run your race the way you can—nor you theirs. Freedom is born when you commit to fighting your way to the finish, because no one can claim your medal but you. Freedom comes when you stop comparing yourself with the person ahead of you or behind you and choose to have a healthy respect for yourself as you put one foot in front of the other.

Stop letting where other people are in their run determine how you feel about your own.

Run your race.

Choose freedom by celebrating your journey, your pace, your finish line.

Don't compare.

Run when you can, walk if you have to, crawl if you must, but never give up.

> Stop letting where other people are in their run determine how you feel about your own.

Reflections for the Rescue

REMEMBER

God will not ask you about how you lived your life in comparison with other people.

REFLECT

- Who do you typically compare yourself with? Name a person or simply a type of person (married, financially secure, driven, thin, etc.)
- Why do you compare yourself? In what areas of your life are you envious of others?
- Take a moment and practice contentment. What's right in your life? What's good about your life today?

RESPOND

Knowing that you are ultimately living for an audience of one, what are your benchmarks? What do *you* want to achieve? Who do *you* want to be? What does God require of you?

Philippians 4:11–13; Luke 12:15;
Matthew 6:25–26; Hebrews 13:5; 1 Timothy 6:6–7;
Proverbs 28:6; Ecclesiastes 3:13.

THE GREAT COVER-UP

Choose Honesty

S elfies.

Most of us have taken them. Some of us have taken them seriously.

If you've ever posted a selfie on social media, you can appreciate the work it takes to get a good one. The lighting has to be right. The angle has to be right. And Lord knows the filter has to be right too.

Selfies are serious business.

I'm embarrassed to say there have been times it took thirty snaps to get the one photo I felt represented what I wanted others to see.

'Cause what others see is important to us.

We might care to varying degrees depending on the people who are looking, but we do care. And that can be the problem.

Most of us have snapshots of our lives we don't care for others to see. We prefer to present that one picture taken in the right light, at the right angle, and with the right filter. Yet when we care too much, it makes us unwilling to be vulnerable and authentic. And so we choose instead to edit out the parts of ourselves we don't want others to see.

We enter into the great cover-up.

We trick ourselves into believing that saving face is more important than saving our girl. We manipulate our mindsets into thinking that keeping up a good front matters more than staying faithful to the process and the product of a focused life. We pretend we aren't hurting or that our lives don't feel overwhelmingly hard. We pretend we haven't made mistakes or that we haven't failed—or failed *again*.

We cover up that we feel like we're shrinking on the inside by wearing a smile and convincing everyone we're okay, and we keep shrinking.

We cover up that our marriage—the marriage everyone thought was perfect—is rife with problems, and we keep struggling.

We cover up that we feel lonely and are longing to be known, and we continue to live in isolation.

We cover up that we really aren't good with God by being good at religion, and we remain distant, detached, and disinterested.

We cover up that our streak of sobriety ended with one glass, and we slide rapidly into past patterns of overindulging.

We cover up that we're struggling with purity, and we back right into the corner of shame, self-condemnation, and guilt, which only keeps us sleeping around.

The cover-up can kill your commitment. It can suffocate you and cease your participation in the very process that will save your life. Just like that girl in the garden of Eden, our first instinct is to cover up our mistakes, to hide our faults, frustrations, and shame. Our greatest cover-ups happen when we convince ourselves that if no one can see our struggle, then it's not real.

> **The cover-up can kill your commitment. It can suffocate you and cease your participation in the very process that will save your life.**

If and when you choose to dig deep and live with focus, you will have multiple opportunities to shortcut the process of honoring your life. You may never get around to taking action. You might tire of the attention it requires to live an authentic life. You could let down your guard and not judge people, places, and things correctly. The struggle with the consistency necessary to exercise ongoing discipline on your journey may entice you to throw up your hands and cry uncle.

You also may be tempted to disguise defeat by wearing a mask.

"I am okay."

That's what I told myself as I pulled my one pair of Old Navy Sweetheart jeans from my closet. 'Cause you know, the other three pairs of jeans hanging in there had grown too small and weren't an option.

Totally not my fault.

I told myself I was okay as I forcefully pulled those jeans over my hips, then almost fainted from exhaling a ton of air to suck in my stomach and button them closed. I told myself I was okay when I saw the extra fat spilling out over the waistband and covered it up with a flowing, forgiving top.

But a little later, in a rush to get to the airport and catch my flight, I stepped up and into my SUV and heard a loud *riiiiip!*

In this moment, I was forced to admit to myself that I was not all-the-way okay.

I looked down to see the *huge* tear in my jeans—right where the turn of my upper inner leg connected with my back thigh. I froze for a second, trying to come up with a plan. Looking over my shoulder, I checked to see who else might have seen my situation or heard the sound of denim tearing.

I didn't have time to fix it. I was rushing to catch my flight, and there was no spare second to change. I could only hope that people might think I was a nineteen-year-old who had an on-purpose tear in her pants. You know, the kind that people actually pay extra money for because it's supposed to mean something great about their fashion sense. If that plan failed, I resigned to let people whisper about me and wonder if I knew my jeans had a gaping hole in them.

Yep. I knew.

But I had to catch that plane, so instead of dealing with my tear, I just kept moving and chose to live vicariously through the unavoidable opportunity presented to me to show some skin. I decided to accept my situation as the best I could do at the moment and pursue a solution as soon as I could.

As soon as my plane landed, I headed straight for an Old Navy to buy a new pair of Sweetheart jeans in the next size up. It was easier to cover my patootie than to deal with the problem of the tear.

Yup. I know I told you at the beginning of our journey together that you are okay, but even if you're good at being okay (and I want you to be) and accepting where you are at the moment, don't get comfortable in the cover-up. When something goes wrong—when you drop the ball, when you lose focus or make a mistake—you get to choose how you handle that moment. You could cover it up and move forward as if the tear never happened or the reason for the tear doesn't matter. It might feel better in the moment to hope no one sees the problem, then work as fast as you can to smooth things over without ever dealing with what caused the problem in the first place.

We don't like being seen.

We don't like to show people our tears. We don't want others to know about our poor decisions, our misdirection, or our lack of discernment. We don't want other people to know that we lack discipline.

The great cover-up happens when we become more concerned with protecting our image than we are with fixing the problem. So the problem persists. We can do such a good job of hiding our tears from others that we do a good job of hiding them from ourselves. When left unattended, the embarrassment, guilt, shame, or self-consciousness only grows bigger, and the more we hide, the more there is to keep hiding.

Shame grows in secret.

To continue moving forward, you have to make up your mind to live in the light, to be honest with yourself about your tears, and then be vulnerable and authentic with others. Once you realize that something in your life has taken you off the path of decision, direction, discernment, and discipline and thrown you into a ditch, don't settle for staying there. In the words of Beth Moore, "Get out of that pit!"

> Shame grows
> in secret.

Find a safe place, and take off the mask.

Reject the disguise, and be willing to be known.

Don't persist in the cover-up. Don't avoid the process of your progress. Deal with your tears. Coach your thoughts, feelings, and actions from the perspective of truth. Do the work of processing your pain.

Because I have felt great pain and because I have had to be strong to get through hard seasons of my life, I learned early to cover up well. That cover-up led to years of making the same mistakes—followed by even bigger mistakes to cover up the mess-ups—and sliding down the slippery slope of lying to myself about my reality. I'm telling you from experience that the great cover-up only hurts you.

You've got to own your story. You must acknowledge the drifts, decisions, and collisions that have put you where you are. Choose to look at your life through the lens of a God who loves you dearly and you will see what there is in you to celebrate. Cultivate your soul, stay open to joy, deal with your pain, and then dig deep, focus, and commit to the process of progress.

But even if you do all of that, though, you will—at some point—fall short.

It's the plight of the human condition.

We all fall short.

But when you fall, when you see your faults or experience a tear, don't settle for the great cover-up.

Take off the mask, the one you've been hiding behind for a long time, and know that when you do, it can hurt. The light burns, and the fresh air feels uncomfortable. Acknowledging your tears leaves you open to criticism and judgment by those who have no idea what it means to walk in your shoes.

> Find a safe place, and take off the mask. Reject the disguise, and be willing to be known.

But in the process, you open yourself up to freedom.

When you reject the great cover-up, you also reject a weight that's kept you burdened by a lie you don't have to continue living with. When you take off the mask, acknowledge your tears, and reject the cover-up, you will be able to breathe.

You will live in the light, acknowledge your tears, reject the weight, and live free.

Reflections for the Rescue

REMEMBER

Don't get comfortable in the cover-up.

REFLECT

- Take a moment to think about what you may be hiding. What do you not want people to know? Why are you afraid to be known?
- How is the cover-up working for you? What has happened in your head and in your heart as you hide guilt, shame, embarrassment, or self-consciousness?
- What do you think it will look like for you to live in the light? Who will help you take off the mask? When?

RESPOND

Name a person and name a date. Be brave and hold yourself to your unmasking.

---

1 John 1:6–10; Isaiah 43:18–19; Romans 8:1; Hebrews 8:12;
Psalm 32:5; James 5:16; Proverbs 28:13; Romans 3:23;
Matthew 7:5; Colossians 1:21–22; Acts 19:18.

CHAPTER 29

THE SISTER CIRCLE

Choose Community

There's an intriguing documentary on Netflix about world champion tennis players Venus and Serena Williams. I've watched it four times so far.

It's so interesting to me how two girls from the same family can both be world champions. I'm fascinated by the dynamics of their upbringing, their training, and their path to success. But more than anything, I'm fascinated by the dynamics of their relationship.

These girls are sisters. They both desire to be at the top of their game, but that also means they regularly compete against each other. But while each girl shows up with a strong desire to come home with the first-place trophy, her fight for first does not trump this most important truth: they are sisters. Those two girls love each other deeply, and each wants to see the other succeed.

In one scene of the documentary, a reporter asks Venus how she feels after Serena beats her in a match. Venus replies, "Of course I want to win, but at the end of the day, both of us share the same last name. Serena is my sister. If one of us wins, we both win."[19]

Because these girls are sisters, they don't let competition define their relationship. They challenge and coach each other. They serve (pun intended) and support one another. They give each other the freedom to pursue individual goals while making sure that they face the world together.

They are sisters.

They know they have their own games to play, but they don't forget the importance of accountability, motivation, and love in their relationship.

That's what sisters do.

They share.

They hold each other's hand.

They encourage.

I have shed blood, sweat, and tears pouring my heart into this book for you because I'm your sister.

While I've got my own battles to face and my own life to live, I know how important it is for you to have a cheerleader, someone who is fighting for your life even while she is fighting for her own.

But here's the reality. As much as I would love to continue this conversation with you over a weekly cup of coffee, you need a sister in your *real* life who is willing to be your champion while you also champion her.

We were not meant to journey through this life alone. Find someone in your world who can encourage you (real life is best, but virtual will do). Find someone whom you can encourage. Hold her hand. Tell your story.

Your sister circle may not come to you. You may have to create it. You may need to be the sister you want to have. You may need to seek out women with whom you can be authentic, transparent, and real in order to fight for the win in your life. You may need to be

> **We were not meant to journey through this life alone.**

more intentional with the existing relationships you have and move from sharing casual experiences to having deep conversations that evoke accountability and real change. You may need to reject the competitive and petty comparisons that define some of your female relationships and get down to the real business of loving well the women God has placed in your path.

I want to challenge you to create a sister circle—a group of friends who are committed to being your cheerleaders. You need other women in your life who are willing to fight for the girl in you even while they are fighting for the girl in them.

You don't have to have a large circle of sisters to know the beauty of support, compassion, or even tough love. We are all busy, and maintaining friendships over coffee on a weekly basis may not be a reasonable expectation. But you *can* be a good friend to one or two people, calling, texting, or showing up to let them know you are in their corner. Never forget that the gift given to you by God can also be a gift to someone else. Even if you have a little living under your belt, the person who is a few steps behind you needs you.

What do you do after finishing this book?

Do what I will be doing.

> **Never forget that the gift given to you by God can also be a gift to someone else.**

When I finish sharing my heart with you in this book, I will go back to loving well on the sisters in my circle. I wish that I could spend one-on-one time with each one of you, listening, encouraging, and charging you up. But I wouldn't be a good friend to anyone if I did that for everyone. And neither would you.

So commit to at least one or two women in your life. Strive for long-haul relationships, the kind that are deep and real. Take the development of the sisters in your circle seriously. Celebrate your sister. Support her as she runs her race. Be a safe place for her to take off her mask.

Move forward in life while keeping an eye on your sister to make sure she's moving too.

Live knowing that we are ultimately alive not for ourselves but for one another.

Believe in the concept of community.

And know this: when she wins, you both win.

Reflections for the Rescue

REMEMBER

Believe in the concept of community.

REFLECT

- As you read this chapter, what feelings or thoughts came to mind about your own sister circle?
- If you don't have a sister circle, think about who or where your sister circle might be. What women do you naturally have the opportunity to be around? Where might you share common backgrounds, life season, interests, or location? If you have one, think about who you may need to invite into your circle. Be open if God puts someone on your mind.
- How can you be more intentional about encouraging your sister friends to honor their lives? How can your friends help you to honor your own? When is the last time you talked or got together?

RESPOND

Take time right now to text one or two of your girls and set a time to talk or meet up. Friendship matters.

Hebrews 10:24–25; Psalm 133:1; 1 Peter 3:8; Matthew 18:20;
Colossians 3:14; 1 John 4:11; 1 John 3:16–17.

THE BUTTERFLY EFFECT

Dare to Believe Change Is Possible

B ecause I homeschool my kids, I get the sheer pleasure of being their teacher for all subjects.

Even the ones I don't particularly like.

Science is not my thing. I have issues with the experiments. They don't work or I'm missing some needed item or the experiment is a little messy or straight-up gross.

I don't mind experiments in general. I just don't want to be in charge of them.

But there's one experiment I've done three times now that I kind of enjoy.

The butterfly garden.

This experiment is more like an experience. We culminate our year of kindergarten science by watching caterpillars turn into butterflies.

I most recently did this experiment with my youngest son. When I gathered all the books and supplies he needed for the school year, he saw the box for the butterfly garden and was excited to know that this year he'd have his turn with the experience. He spent all year talking about it, and when the time came in early spring, we sent for our caterpillars via mail order.

When the caterpillars arrived, they came in a closed container. No mess for me. Hallelujah.

For a few days, we watched those caterpillars move around the covered plastic cup ever so slowly. Eating, crawling, and eating some more. For a little over a week, the caterpillars stayed in constant, steady-yet-slow motion, but to my little kindergartener son, nothing was happening.

He was looking for a butterfly.

At his age, he understood the concept of time, but each day seemed like an eternity to him, especially when he was looking forward to seeing the butterfly emerge from its chrysalis and fly around our little netted garden in all its glory.

The process of the caterpillar turning into a butterfly was simply taking too long. So long he started to wonder if the transformation would ever happen.

"Mom, are you *sure* that these caterpillars are going to turn into butterflies?"

"Yes, baby. I'm sure."

Next day. Same question. Different format.

"Mom, why aren't the caterpillars turning into butterflies? *How long* is this gonna take?"

"Son, they will turn into butterflies. It'll just take a little while longer."

A few days later, the butterflies made their way to the top of the plastic container and hung from the lid. Within twenty-four hours, the chrysalises had formed and the caterpillars were perfectly still and seemingly lifeless.

"Mom, are the caterpillars dead?"

"No son, they aren't dead. They're turning into butterflies."

"But Mom, *nothing's happening!*"

I could totally see why my son would think that.

It didn't look like anything *was* happening. After days of slow movement, the caterpillars had hidden away, become totally still, and nothing appeared to be happening at all.

But I had a vantage point that my son didn't have.

Because I had done this experiment before with my two older sons, I knew what to expect. I'd experienced the process. I knew that the transformation he wanted to see would take some time, and that patience would be required.

I knew if my kindergartner could just hold on a little while longer, he would see butterflies emerge. He just needed to hang in there and believe.

It took a while, but we watched, faithfully expecting something beautiful to be born.

When nothing was happening, we watched.

When the change was taking forever, we watched.

When there was no movement, we watched.

We watched, waited, and eventually witnessed the miracle of metamorphosis.

The butterfly slowly but surely made its way out of the chrysalis, struggling to break free from all that had constrained it but also all that would create its beauty. And from that struggle, the butterfly gained the strength it needed to fly.

I know that as I've shared my heart with you in this book, you might easily be able to believe me because you've been through your own process and seen what happens when you hang in there and hold on to hope for the life of the girl in you. I hope you've been encouraged, inspired, and motivated to live with a clear vision of the beautiful soul God has given you.

But I also know that you might be like my son, wanting to see changes, but frustrated that those changes in your life are happening so slowly—or don't appear to be happening at all.

You might be wondering how long a transformation in your life is going to take, and whether the change you hope to see will ever happen.

You might be wondering if God sees you—if He knows that you feel buried deep down below the surface of what should be your life and if He actually intends to help you make your way there.

You might very well want to see yourself operating in the fullness and beauty of the girl God created you to be, but because you still struggle or because change is happening slowly or because no one watching your life appears to believe in your life, you may not be sure a life that matters is within your reach.

You may be like my son and find yourself hesitant to believe because you've never seen it before. You may not ever have seen the process completed in your own life or even in the life of someone you know.

But I have.

So I'd like to ask you to trust me.

I'd like to ask you to believe that since I've seen it in my own life and in the lives of others, a transformation is possible for you.

I'd like to ask you to believe that even if the road is rough and your story is messy, the way your world looks today is not how it has to look tomorrow.

I'd like to ask you to believe that even while your progress may seem slow, if you remain faithful in doing the work required by the season you're in, you're doing the perfect work to rescue the girl in you.

But I'm also asking you to embrace the struggle.

I want to challenge you to embrace the process of your progress and to focus on pouring yourself fully into making the decisions you need to make, and then doing whatever it takes to stick with your chosen direction. I hope you'll use discernment in the people, places, and things that are in your life, and that you'll exercise the discipline necessary to dig deep and get to the girl you were always meant to be.

I'm praying as I write this chapter that when the process of your progress gets too hard, feels too long, or seems to cost too much, you'll do what it takes to coach yourself back to the truths you believe. And

I pray that you'll celebrate along the way, showing gratitude for small accomplishments, little victories, and every baby step you take. I'm also hoping you'll put more effort into focusing on your own two feet than comparing yourself with the people around you.

And if you fall, I'm cheering for you to get back up, own your story, and continue on your journey, resisting the cover-up that often accompanies shame and guilt.

I invite you to live your life—being, believing, and becoming the person God knew you could be when he planted His gifts in you.

I want you to embrace and expect that your process will probably not be perfect, but trust that God can use even your drifts, decisions, and collisions as soil in which something beautiful can grow and bloom.

Most important, I hope you see now that even beautiful lives—*especially* beautiful lives—require work.

> God can use even your drifts, decisions, and collisions as soil in which something beautiful can grow and bloom.

I hope you understand that there's no shortcut to doing the work of nourishing your soul, taking care of your body, and participating with the work of God's Spirit in you. While you need to know truth and understand truth, you have to do the work of operating in truth, however long it takes or however difficult that process might be. Every bit of your process and all the work you put in will be worth it when you see the beauty that emerges in you as you partner with God's design and plan for your life.

———

Beautiful girl, every struggle you have will help you develop the strength you need to fly. You are capable of doing the work. You have the right to hope and dream. And I want excitement to bubble up in you as you realize that you, my friend, get a turn.

I am asking you to believe in the butterfly effect that is at work in you.

Wait for it.

Watch for it.

Work for it.

Hope for it.

Pray for it.

Dare to believe. Change is possible.

And this is what I know for sure about the girl you want to be or the girl you didn't know you could be: she's still there.

～～⌒〇

Well, I can't describe her exactly—
except to say that she was beautiful.
She was—tremendously alive.

—F. Scott Fitzgerald

Reflections for the Rescue

REMEMBER

Every struggle you have will help you develop the strength you need.

REFLECT

- What is your next step after reading this book? What are you motivated to do?
- What thoughts or actions do you need to change today to consistently honor the life of the girl in you?
- What is your dream for the girl in you? What are you daring to believe?

RESPOND

Seal the deal. Take time to marinate on the message of this book *for you*. Journal about your dreams, make a list of your goals, or pray about the next steps. Be motivated enough to take action. Then share your plan of action with a sister friend.

Psalm 51:10; Ezekiel 36:26; 2 Corinthians 3:17–18;
2 Corinthians 5:17; Ephesians 4:23–24; Titus 3:5;
Romans 8:29; Romans 12:2.

CLOSING
THOUGHTS FOR
MY READER

I love Jesus.

I love Him for many reasons, but most of all because He first loved me.

I wrote this book assuming that you love Him too, but I don't want to end our coffee conversation without making sure you understand how *much* He loves you.

You aren't the only one who's ever felt lost or messed up or drifted away from all that is right and good. We all sin. We all miss the mark. And because He is perfect, our faults separate us from Him.

No matter how hard we work to play our part in our own rescue, we will always fall short. There is nothing we can do—no amount of good we can achieve—that will measure up to His standard of righteousness.

The good news is He didn't just give you the gift of "you." He knew you would need more than that to experience life to the fullest. Because our sin separates us from Him forever, He knew that you and I would need a partner in the rescue effort. He knew we would need someone who could reach down and give us the help we need to get back above ground and stay there.

So He became the gift. God wrapped himself in a human body and lived a perfect life on earth for you and for me.

He knew that we would not be able to live with impeccable goodness a hundred percent of the time. And since the only way to have a relationship with the God of the Universe is perfection, He sacrificed His perfect life for us.

He died. He willingly gave up His life because that was the only way you and I could live, live with Him, and live forever.

The only thing you have to do to experience an abundant life now and to have life forever is to accept His gift by believing that Jesus died in your place to rescue you from the effects of your sin. It's that simple.

The best part is He didn't stay buried. He got up out of the grave and is alive today. He is a master of the art of the rescue and would love for you to trust Him to help you in your own.

You simply have to invite Him to do so.

Would you like to know more about what it means to trust in Jesus Christ for your rescue effort?

Visit *chrystalevanshurst.com/tellmemore*. I'd love to show you the Way.

GAIN A NEW PERSPECTIVE

Personal Assessment

What Are Your Gifts?

IDEAS TO GET YOU GOING: Are you musically inclined or athletically gifted? Maybe you're highly analytical and good with numbers? Do you see possibilities that no one else seems to see? Maybe you are a visionary and comfortable taking risks. Do you have a natural way with people? Are you naturally a peacemaker? Do you enjoy resolving conflict or do you run from it? Are you an effective listener? Or maybe you are good with words. Are you particularly good with the written word? Does verbal communication flow from your mouth? Do you have a way with children? Do you have never-ending creative ideas? Maybe you are good at motivating others.

What types of activities come easily for you?

What do you have a natural capacity for that isn't always natural for others?

What seems to click for you?

What do you do effortlessly that doesn't seem to be so simple for others?

What Are Your Abilities?

IDEAS TO GET YOU GOING: What skill do you have? What have you learned to do? Are you a good manager? Do you have developed artistic skill? Can you teach? Can you cook? Can you design graphics? Do you have beautiful handwriting? Can you repair mechanical equipment? Do you counsel others? Are you able to effectively strategize or organize information, people, or events? Can you sew? Do you have a green thumb? Are you a whiz with computer programs?

What have you learned to do?

What knowledge do you have?

What special training have you received?

In what area have you had lots of practice or experience?

What could you do with your eyes closed because you've been doing it so long?

What can you do because you watched someone else do it?

What Are Your Interests or Passions?

IDEAS TO GET YOU GOING: Maybe you love to read or love spending time with people. Interested in a sport? Maybe you can't get enough of decorating magazines or visits to the craft store. Are you the kind of person who gets a great deal of satisfaction from balancing your checkbook to the penny? What about working with your hands? Do you have a knack for fixing or building things? Does having friends over for an evening meal make you want to squeal with delight? Do you like working with people who need a helping hand? How about seeing new places and experiencing new things? Are you a queen of research? Do you like figuring things out?

What do you enjoy doing?

What do you want to learn more about?

What sets your soul on fire?

Without the interruption of technology or social media, what interests would you give time to developing, practicing, or doing if you don't have to?

What interests or passions bubble up whether you cultivate them or not?

Think about Your Nature!

IDEAS TO GET YOU GOING: Are you honest, driven, or loyal? Are you particularly kind, thoughtful, or caring? What about words like curious, cooperative, or flexible? Adaptable or adventuresome? Affectionate or ambitious? Have you proven that you are brave or confident? Stable or thorough? Responsible or self-disciplined? Fun or easygoing?

What *positive* words would you use to describe your personality or character?

GAIN a New Perspective

IDEAS TO GET YOU GOING: Hopeful or disappointed? Happy or hurt? Bold or bored? Courageous or careful? Glass half full or half empty? Too fast or too slow? Overwhelmed or peaceful? Hard or easygoing?

- Take a moment to look over the things that you have uncovered about yourself. Appreciate who you are right now, and thank God for the raw material he's given you.

- Now, let's take a look at your perspective. What words would you use to illustrate your attitude about your life? If you could sum up your attitude about your life in one or two words, what would those words be?

Good for you for sticking with me this far. Looking at your life is work. It takes time. And frankly many of us don't do it for that very reason. Kudos to you for giving yourself the gift of looking and listening.

Now here's your final challenge. I want you to create a value statement that contains both honesty and encouragement about your life right now. Fill in the blanks:

Right now, I look at my life and see/feel/think:

_____

(insert two to three words from the current assessment of your life)

But I am good at:

_____

(describe your gifts)

And I am capable of:

_____

(describe your abilities)

I enjoy:

_____

(list your areas of interest or passion)

And I know that I am:

_____

(describe your nature, character, or personality)

So regardless of how I feel, I choose today to honor God with my life and use my gift in my world.

Next Steps

- Ask people who care about you to help you complete the assessment.
- Honor who you are by remembering whose you are.
- Pick at least one attribute from your GAIN list and do it, explore it, or use it.

Taking the time to GAIN a new perspective gave me a great start and has continued to motivate me in partnering with God to structure my life around my design. I believe that you will find that it will do the same for you.

NOTES

1. "Baby Jessica Biography," *Biography.com*, April 2, 2014, http://www .biography.com/people/baby-jessica-17175736. Accessed November 2016.
2. Brene Brown, *The Gifts of Imperfection* (Center City, MN: Hazelden Publishing, 2010), 6.
3. Katherine Preston, "Owning Your Own Story," *PyschologyToday.com*, January 16, 2014, https://www.psychologytoday.com/blog/out-it/ 201401/owning-your-own-story. Accessed November 2016.
4. Gretchen Rubin, "Quiz: Are You Drifting?" *GretchenRubin.com*, July 22, 2009, http://gretchenrubin.com/happiness_project/2009/07/ quiz-are-you-drifting/. Accessed November 2016.
5. Maria Popva, "The Shortness of Life: Seneca on Busyness and the Art of Living Wide Rather Than Living Long," *BrainPickings.org*, (n.d.), https://www.brainpickings.org/2014/09/01/seneca-on-the-shortness -of-life/. Accessed January 2017.
6. Nicholas Bakalar, "37.2 Trillion: Galaxies or Human Cells?" *New York Times*, June 19, 2015, https://www.nytimes.com/2015/06/23/science/ 37-2-trillion-galaxies-or-human-cells.html. Accessed January 2017.
7. Sandee LaMotte, "The Other 'Fingerprints' You Don't Know About," *CNN.com*, December 4, 2015, http://www.cnn.com/2015/12/04/ health/unique-body-parts/index.html. Accessed November 2016.
8. Joyce Meyer, *How to Succeed at Being Yourself* (New York: Warner Faith, 2002), 19.

9. Sarah Bowling, *In Heavenly Help: Experiencing the Holy Spirit in Everyday Life* (Grand Rapids: Chosen Books, 2016), 69.

10. Mary Oliver, "The Summer Day," in *New and Selected Poems*, vol. 1 (Boston: Beacon, 2004), 94.

11. "Henri Nouwen Quotes," *AZQuotes.com*, (n.d.), http://www.azquotes .com/author/10905-Henri_Nouwen. Accessed January 2017.

12. Jill Becker, "Shaping Sara Blakely: Meet the Billionaire Founder of Spanx," *Success.com*, December 7, 2015, http://www.success.com/article/ shaping-sara-blakely-meet-the-billionaire-founder-of-spanx. Accessed January 2017.

13. Naomi Blumberg, "Misty Copeland: American Dancer," *Encyclopaedia Britannica*, October 5, 2016, https://www.britannica.com/biography/ Misty-Copeland. Accessed January 2017.

14. "Lee Iacocca Quotes," *BrainyQuote.com*, (n.d.), http://www.brainyquote .com/quotes/quotes/l/leeiacocca149249.html. Accessed November 2016.

15. Brian Wansink, *Mindless Eating: Why We Eat More Than We Think* (New York: Bantam Dell, 2006), 29.

16. "Jennifer Hudson Quotes," *AZQuotes.com*, (n.d.), http://www.azquotes .com/author/6993-Jennifer_Hudson.

17. Denzel Washington, director, *The Great Debaters* (motion picture), 2007.

18. Steven Furtick, *@stevenfurtick*, May 10, 2011, https://twitter.com/ stevenfurtick/status/67981913746444288. Accessed November 2016.

19. Maiken Baird and Michelle Major, directors, *Venus and Serena* (motion picture), Magnolia Pictures, 2012.